Italian Instrumental Music of the Sixteenth and Early Seventeenth Centuries

Previously unpublished full scores of major works
from the Renaissance and Early Baroque

Selected and Edited by
JAMES LADEWIG
University of Rhode Island

A Garland Series

VOLUME 24

Giovanni Antonio Cangiasi

Scherzi forastieri per suonare a quattro voci
(Milan, 1614)

Edited by
ROBERT JUDD
California State University–Fresno

GARLAND PUBLISHING, INC.
NEW YORK & LONDON 1991

Copyright © 1991 Robert Judd

Library of Congress Cataloging-in-Publication Data

Cangiasi, Giovanni Antonio, d. 1614?
    Scherzi forastieri: per suonare a quattro voci (Milan, 1614) / Giovanni Antonio Cangiasi: edited by Robert Judd.
    1 score.—(Italian instrumental music of the sixteenth and early seventeenth centuries: v. 24)
    Canzonas for 4 unspecified instruments (canto, alto, tenore, basso).
    1. Quartets (Unspecified instruments (4))—Scores. I. Judd, Robert. II. Title. III. Series.
    M990.C32S3   1991   91-751636
    ISBN 0-8240-4523-8 (alk. paper)

The volumes in this series have been printed on acid-free, 250-year-life paper.

Printed in the United States of America.

CONTENTS

General Introduction	ix
Editorial Methods	xi
Introduction to this Volume	xiii
1. *Canzon prima, L'Obligata*	1
Alla Nobilissima Communità di Castelnuovo di Scrivia	
2. *Canzon seconda, La Consigliata*	9
All'Illustre Conseglio di Castelnuovo di Scrivia	
3. *Canzon terza, La Marina*	16
All'Illustre Signor, il Sig. Girolamo Marini, Marchese Dignissimo di Castelnuovo di Scrivia	
4. *Canzon quarta, La Marina*	23
Al Molto Illustre Signor, il Sig. Filippo Marini, Marchese Dignissimo di Castelnuovo di Scrivia	
5. *Canzon quinta, La Stella*	29
All'Illustr. & Eccell. Sig. il Sig. Sebastian Stella, Dottore dell'una, e l'altra legge	

6. *Canzon sesta, La Bussola*   35
       All'Illust. & Eccell. Sign. il Sig.
       Ubaldo Bussola, Dottore dell'una,
       e l'altra Legge

7. *Canzon settima, La Grassa*   41
       All'Illust. & Eccell. Sig. il Sig.
       Alessandro Grasso, Dottore dell'una,
       e l'altra legge

8. *Canzon ottava, La Grassa*   48
       All'Illust. & Eccell. Sig. il Sig.
       Francesco Grasso, Dottore dell'una,
       e l'altra legge

9. *Canzon nona, La Theorica*   56
       All'Illust. & Eccell. Sign. il Sig.
       Aurelio Bussola, Lettore di Theorica,
       Medicina Ordinaria nel Studio di Pavia

10. *Canzon decima, La Guerra*   63
       All'Illustre Sig. il Sig. Viscardo Guerra

11. *Canzon undecima, La Capitania*   70
       All'Illust. Sign. il Sig. Lodrico Basso,
       Capitan' Valorosissimo

12. *Canzon duodecima, La Bassa*   79
       Al Molto Illustre Sig. il Sig.
       Girolamo Bassi

13. *Canzon decimaterza, La Torta*   89
       All'Ill. Sig. il Sig. Dario Torto

14. *Canzon decimaquarta, La Filippa*   96
    All'Illust. e Molto Reverendo Sig.
    il Sig. Filippo Grasso, Prevosto
    Dignissimo di Castelnuovo di Scrivia

15. *Canzon decimaquinta, La Fiorina*   103
    All'Illust. Sign. il Sign. Camillo
    Campeggio

16. *Canzon decimasesta, La Girometta*   112
    All'Ill. Sig. il Sig. Giovanni Moro

17. *Canzon decimasettima, La Genovesa*   120
    Alli Molto RR. PP. e Maestri del
    Convento di S. Francesco, Minori
    Conventuali di Genova

18. *Canzon decimaottava, La Alessandrina*   128
    All'Illust. Sig. il Sig. Alessandro Basso

19. *Canzon decimanona, La Confrata*   135
    Alla Vener. Compagnia de Signori
    Confrati di S. Rocho di Castelnuovo
    di Scrivia

20. *Canzon vigesima, La Furugada*   142
    Alla Nobile, e Virtuosa Gioventù
    di Castelnuovo di Scrivia

21. *Canzon vigesimaprima, La Pessa*   153
    Di Fra Bonaventura Pessa suo Discepolo
    Al M. R. P. Gio. Antonio Cangiasi,
    Maestro di Musica, & Organista
    Eccellentissimo

GENERAL INTRODUCTION

Sixteenth-century Italy witnessed one of the greatest flowerings of instrumental music in Western culture. This series presents over six hundred pieces contained in thirty-seven publications of Italian instrumental ensemble music dating from the middle of the sixteenth century through the first three decades of the seventeenth century. A broad sampling of publications has been chosen to provide a representative cross section of the leading composers, chronological development, important geographical centers, and varied styles and genres of this repertory.

By the middle of the sixteenth century, Italy had become the leading center in the production of instrumental music, including that for lute, keyboard, and instrumental ensemble. The landmark publication of ensemble music was *Musica nova* of 1540, containing the earliest imitative ricercars for instrumental consort by Adrian Willaert, Julio Segni, and others.[1] This volume opened the way for a steady stream of ensemble ricercars, canzonas, dances, and the like, which Italian printers continued to issue well into the early seventeenth century. The two most highly esteemed genres of Italian instrumental ensemble music were the ricercar and canzona, both of which embraced the equal-voiced counterpoint and pervading imitative texture so characteristic of sixteenth-century vocal music. The ricercar adopted an intensely serious style akin to that of contemporary sacred music, and it accordingly cultivated highly intellectual contrapuntal devices, including inversion, stretto, augmentation, diminution, and ostinato.

The canzona, on the other hand, found its direct inspiration in the Parisian chanson and retained that genre's animated rhythmic style, jocular approach to imitation, and penchant for clearly articulated sectional forms. For a good half century, the ricercar and its close relative, the fantasia, predominated in ensemble publications. Only in 1582 did the first volume of ensemble canzonas appear, the *Libro primo de canzoni da sonare* of Florentio Maschera. By 1600, however, the production of canzonas had clearly outstripped that of ricercars, and after that date the ensemble ricercar quickly declined in popularity. Providing a counterpoise to the high polyphony of the ricercar and canzona was dance music. Unlike the Germans and English, Italians rarely wrote their dances for instrumental ensemble, preferring to restrict the performance of this genre to harpsichord, lute, and other plucked string instruments. This series presents a substantial proportion of the relatively small body of Italian ensemble dances by including those of Allegri, Biumi, Cavaccio, and Kapsberger.

The blossoming of the new Baroque style around 1600 created many sudden stylistic upheavals in the realm of vocal music, but in the instrumental genres its development proceeded slowly and gradually. For a while the older style of Renaissance ensemble music written in equal-voiced counterpoint coexisted with the new solo and trio sonatas of the Baroque, characterized by their polarized texture of one or two high parts supported by the newfangled *basso continuo*. Around 1620, a noticeable dwindling began in the number of new publications of equal-voiced instrumental ensemble music, and the genre became virtually extinct by 1630. Ricercars and canzonas did, nonetheless, continue to appear in publications and manuscripts of keyboard music, where, during the course of the seventeenth century, these two genres coalesced into the fugue.

The majority of the music in this series is for four-part instrumental ensemble. Three-part works were also cultivated, especially in the sixteenth century, and often appeared with fanciful titles such as *fantasie*, *capricci*, or *tercetti a note*. In the early seventeenth century, pieces for more than four instruments—especially eight-part polychoral canzonas—came into vogue, inspired by the compositions of Giovanni Gabrieli. Such works are well represented in the series. Omitted, however, are instrumental duos, so-called *bicinie*. Because of their primarily didactic function, such works represent a separate category of instrumental music. Eliminated from the series are pieces in solo- and trio-sonata texture with obligatory *basso continuo*, whereas publications of works for four or more parts accompanied by the more optional *basso seguente* have been included. In two publications of late date, however, we have retained a few pieces in the manner of solo and trio sonatas so as to keep intact publications which otherwise call for *basso seguente*. A significant number of Italian instrumental compositions appear in publications that contain vocal music as well. The vocal works in these publications are omitted from the series when they constitute the greater part of the volume and when the instrumental pieces form a self-contained group of works that can stand alone. On the other hand, vocal compositions that take up only a small portion of a publication are retained, so as to preserve the integrity of the original print.

With this series, a number of publications (including three volumes of *Ricercari* by Merulo and the *Capricci overo canzoni* of Bariolla) which come down to us only in incomplete sets of partbooks now finally appear in modern edition. Their missing parts are supplied from the Turin keyboard manuscripts, where they survive in New German Keyboard Tablature. Two publications that have recently come to light appear herein for the first time in modern edition: Kapsberger's *Libro primo de balli, gagliarde, et correnti* (1615) and the instrumental portion of Grillo's *Sacri concentus ac symphoniae* (1618), the latter of which is closely modelled after Giovanni Gabrieli's famous 1597 volume of similar title. The present editor has located the only surviving complete copy of Giovanni Bassano's *Fantasie a tre voci* (1585). Now housed at the Jagiellonska Library in Krakow, this copy was long believed to have been destroyed during World War II. It appears here for the first time in modern edition in its entirety.

The music in this series may be performed with historical authenticity on a much wider variety of instruments than the nowadays conventional early-music consorts of recorders, violas da gamba, cornetti, sackbuts, and so forth. Keyboard manuscripts of the late sixteenth and early seventeenth centuries, for example, preserve transcriptions of vast quantities of the ensemble repertory.[2] Lutenists, too, frequently adapted this music for their own instrument. Even singers of the time often performed instrumental music directly from the partbooks, adding solmization syllables as they went. This series thus furnishes scholars and a wide spectrum of performers alike with the means for achieving a broader understanding and appreciation of one of the most significant repertories of the late Renaissance and early Baroque eras.

[1] H. Colin Slim, ed., *Musica Nova*, Monuments of Renaissance Music, vol. 1 (Chicago and London, 1964).

[2] See James Ladewig, "Frescobaldi's *Recercari, et canzoni franzese* (1615): A Study of the Contrapuntal Keyboard Idiom in Ferrara, Naples, and Rome, 1580–1620" (Ph.D. dissertation, University of California, Berkeley, 1978), I, 294–301.

EDITORIAL METHODS

The purpose of this series is to provide a large repertory of late sixteenth- and early seventeenth-century Italian instrumental music in clear modern editions that are both practical and faithful to the original sources. Original pitch, "key signatures," and note values are retained; "time signatures" also appear as in the original, unless noted in the Introduction. Editorial comments concerning the sources, the original clefs, coloration, and corrected errors in pitch and rhythm are found in the Introduction. The names of the parts, as given in the original source, appear at the beginning of each work. Variant readings among concordant sources are not indicated. Flats and sharps appear exactly as in the original source. Sharp signs applied to B and E, however, are modernized as naturals.

Instead of providing editorial accidentals, this series encourages performers to recreate the process of adding *musica ficta* that must have occurred routinely during the sixteenth century. Performers knew notes by both their letter names (A to G) and their solmization syllables (ut re mi fa sol la). A pitch was determined not simply by its location on the staff but also by its function in the hexachord system, shown by its solmization syllable. (See Example 1.) The note that we read as B, for example, can be sung as either B-natural or B-flat depending on whether it is solmized as mi or fa; the decision of how to solmize it depends on the musical context. The following is a brief account of the principles of *musica ficta* that guided performers in choosing the correct solmization syllable, or, as we think of it today, in supplying sharps and flats that are missing from the sources. It should be noted, however, that there will be occasions when these guidelines come into direct conflict with one another.

One should generally "add a flat" (i.e., sing the note as fa) in the following situations:

1. To maintain intervals of the perfect fourth, fifth, and octave between voices (i.e., to avoid vertical tritones, diminished fifths, and octaves that create "mi contra fa").

2. To keep melodic intervals of a fourth or a fifth perfect (i.e., to avoid melodic tritones and diminished fifths).

3. When a melody rises a single step beyond the upper range of a hexachord and then returns to that hexachord, the note above the hexachord should be a semitone (i.e., sung as fa). This is the so-called "una nota super la semper est canendum fa" rule. Some theorists imply that there are situations when this convention should not be used (particularly when the melody soon thereafter continues its upward rise and does not involve a real or implied melodic tritone). Most of the time, however, the principle can be invoked.

One should generally "add a sharp":

4. At cadences, where a sixth moves outward to an octave or a third moves inward to a unison. (See Example 2.)

xii • *EDITORIAL METHODS*

5. To the third of a final chord, where necessary, to create a major triad.

For further readings, see Lewis Lockwood, "Musica ficta, §2," *The New Grove Dictionary of Music and Musicians*, ed. Stanley Sadie (London, 1980), XII, 806–08; Margaret Bent, "Diatonic ficta," *Early Music History* 4 (Cambridge, 1984); and Nicholas Routley, "A practical guide to musica ficta," *Early Music* 13 (1985), 59–71.

Example 1

Hexachord on C
ut re mi fa sol la

Hexachord on G
ut re mi fa sol la

Hexachord on F
ut re mi fa sol la

Example 2

INTRODUCTION TO THIS VOLUME

The scant biographical information we have regarding Giovanni Antonio Cangiasi comes from the title pages and dedications to his published volumes. He was born in Milan, although the precise date is unknown. A Franciscan, he was organist at the cathedral of Vercelli in 1590; in 1602 he was at San Francesco, Milan; in 1607 and 1611 he stayed at the Franciscan monastery in Locarno; and as the present volume indicates, by 1614 he was organist of the cathedral of Castelnuovo di Scrivia. He probably died shortly thereafter.[1]

Five surviving publications are devoted entirely to the music of Cangiasi: *Il secondo libro delle canzonette a tre voci* (Milan: Agostino Tradate, 1602); the *Sacrae cantiones tribus vocibus concinendae* (Milan: Agostino Tradate, 1606); the *Psalmodia ecclesiastica concinenda cum quatuor vocibus* (Milan: Melchior Tradate, 1611); the *Melodia sacra quatuor, et quinque vocibus, cum duobis motectis ad modum dialogi, et uno cum canzon francese . . . motectorum vero eiusdem liber secundus* (Milan: Melchior Tradate, 1612); and the present *Scherzi forastieri per suonare, a quattro voci . . . opera ottava* (Milan: Filippo Lomazzo, 1614). In addition, Eitner cites a volume that is now lost: *Li ariosi Magnificat 8 voc.* (Milan: Francesco Tini, 1590)[2]; and a contemporary trade list cites his *Madrigali a 4 v.*, eleven of which may survive in manuscript form.[3] The present *Scherzi forastieri* (*forastieri* = "from abroad; foreign") are the only entirely instrumental works by Cangiasi; like a number of organists of the time, he published nothing for keyboard but directed his compositional energies primarily toward vocal music.[4] The works in *Scherzi forastieri* are the earliest solely instrumental pieces to be termed *scherzo*, but the musical connotations to the word are negligible here, for the pieces are typical canzonas of the period; indeed, Cangiasi uses the word *canzon* to identify them throughout the volume.[5]

An unusual feature of Cangiasi's volume is its relationship to Castelnuovo di Scrivia, a small Lombardian town almost exactly midway between Genoa and Milan, a few miles south of the Po.[6] As Cangiasi explains in the dedication, he is the "foreigner" to whom the title alludes, and wishes to repay his new fellow-residents for their warm welcome by dedicating the volume as a whole to the *communità* and individual pieces to prominent citizens. Nearly all the works are carefully dedicated to civic groups or figures, the titles often reflecting the names of dedicatees, a common feature of Lombardian canzonas.[7] Included are dedications to the town as a whole (no. 1), the town council (no. 2), the two *marchesi* (nos. 3 and 4), the provost of the cathedral (no. 14), and the "noble and virtuous youth" of the town (no. 20). The latter canzona is entitled *La Furugada*, the meaning of which may be related to *furacan*, "hurricane."[8]

The final canzona, *La Pessa*, is identified as a composition by Cangiasi's pupil Fra Bonaventura Pessa, and dedicated by Pessa to Cangiasi. Nothing is known of Pessa beyond this piece. Given such clear correspondences between titles and dedications in the remainder of the collection, it is unusual that the pupil did not name the canzona after the master but himself; the work closely conforms to the style of Cangiasi, and it may be that Cangiasi had more than a little to do with Pessa's final product.

Cangiasi's collection is part of a fairly extended line of instrumental canzonas that originated in and around Milan between 1580 and 1630.[9] Typically, the instrumental canzona comprises multiple sections clearly demarcated by cadences and differing themes. They are written for four "equal voices," i.e., relatively independent parts predominantly in imitative polyphony. With the rise of basso continuo and solo-and-accompaniment texture, the popularity of works like Cangiasi's declined in favor of works for one or two soloists and accompaniment—solo and trio sonatas. Several features indicate the transitional position the volume holds. Strictly speaking, any accompaniment to such canzonas is redundant, and prior to 1604 canzona collections were usually published without accompaniment partbooks; yet soon after the appearance of Lodovico Grossi da Viadana's watershed volume *Cento concerti ecclesiastici* (Venice, 1602), it became obligatory to include a partbook for the accompanist (in one of several possible formats).[10] Cangiasi accordingly provides a *partitura* for accompaniment, which doubles the instrumental parts exactly (see "The Sources for Volume 24," below). Other signs of the mixture of old and new in these works include the following noteworthy features of Cangiasi's canzonas.

Cangiasi's deployment of sectional form and thematic treatment is striking and by no means old-fashioned. Only three of the twenty-one canzonas do not employ thematic variation to some degree: nos. 1, 10, and 11, the forms of which are A-A-B-C-C', A-A-B-C-B-C-Coda, and A-A-B-C-D-B-C-D-Coda, respectively. Thematic variation occurs in a number of ways, most of which are different from a typical keyboard variation canzona.[11] The theme of the fourth section (m. 36) of no. 2 (A-A-B-A'), for example, is rhythmically derived from the opening. Cangiasi's favorite variation pattern is to develop the first theme extensively over two or three sections before moving to new themes; this procedure is evident in twelve works: no. 3 (A-A'-A inverted-A"-A"), where the opening theme is manipulated throughout; no. 5 (A-A'-A"-B-C-C-Coda), mm. 1–22; no. 6 (A-A'-A"-A"'-B-Coda), mm. 1–32; no. 7 (A-A'-B-C-D-E-Coda), mm. 1–20; no. 8 (A-A'-A"-B-C-B), mm. 1–48; no. 12 (A-A'-A"-B-B'-C-Coda), mm. 1–31; no. 15 (A-A'-A"-A"'-B), mm. 1–27; no. 16 (through-composed variations on the "Girometta" theme), throughout; nos. 18 and 19 (see below); no. 20 (A-A'-B-C-D-E), mm. 1–11; and no. 21 (A-A'-A"-B-C-D), mm. 1–26. Nos. 18 and 19 are essentially ricercars based on one theme that is varied throughout; coupled with nos. 3 and 16, four works use only one theme. No. 19 employs particularly sophisticated counterpoint: stretto, inversion, and diminution. No. 15 is noteworthy for its extended development of the second theme as well as the first (mm. 27–60); similarly, no. 12 develops the C idea extensively (mm. 34–58). No. 14 (A-B-C-A'-A"-Coda) is unusual in developing the A theme over an extended period (mm. 31–60) *after* introducing new thematic material.

Three works stand out from the rest of the collection. The opening of no. 12, *La Bassa*, is based on a descending chromatic line through the tetrachord, which gives way in m. 24 to interesting and unusual *passaggi* in pairs and echo.[12] No. 16, *La Girometta*, likewise takes an interesting theme, the popular song "Girometta," and handles the material with "elegance and imagination."[13] The monothematic work is interrupted by violinistic *passaggi* in mm. 33–35 and echo effects in mm. 38–40; the triple-meter section (m. 48) presents another variation of the melody. No. 20, *La Furugada*, resembles a *battaglia* after the opening two themes: mm. 17–60 present a series of static harmonies articulated with many repeated notes, triad outlines, motives, and cuckoo-figures. The colorful piece is surely intended to be performed at break-neck speed, perhaps for the delight of the youths to whom it is dedicated.

Cangiasi also uses a number of noteworthy small-scale compositional devices: frequent stretto, instrumentally oriented voice-pairs, and a texture consisting of three parts with an independent bass line (e.g., no. 6). In common with many canzonas by other composers, he often uses a "cascading" descending stepwise quarter-note theme in stretto for concluding sections (nos. 3, 5, 11, 16). Effective downbeat rests are found in no. 2, m. 40, and no. 15, mm. 30–31. He uses *inganno* twice: in no. 6, the opening theme; and no. 18, mm. 36–37, *basso*, a subsidiary theme (cf. mm. 34–35, *alto*, and mm. 40–41, *alto*). A "Neapolitan sixth" chord occurs in no. 6, m. 15, a rare sonority before the time of Carissimi.

Unusual or modern dissonance treatment can be found in no. 11, m. 37 (sixth, fifth, and fourth above the bass simultaneously); no. 13, m. 16 (major third and minor sixth above the bass simultaneously); and no. 20, m. 36, which appears to be a double-leading-note cadence. Striking cross-relations occur in no. 11, mm. 5 and 19, and no. 12, mm. 18 and 41.

Freedoms generally regarded as contrapuntal flaws also occur. For example, irregular six-four sonorities occur in no. 13, mm. 37, 41, 42, and 43, and no. 19, m. 21. Parallel perfect intervals on consecutive strong beats occur regularly, e.g., no. 13, m. 37, no. 14, m. 46, and no. 16, m. 23.

THE SOURCES FOR VOLUME 24

This edition of Giovanni Antonio Cangiasi's *Scherzi forastieri* is based on the complete set of partbooks and *partitura* that survives in Verona, Biblioteca Capitolare. An *alto* partbook is extant in Bologna, Biblioteca del Conservatorio, and a *canto* partbook is extant in Berkeley, University of California Music Library. The partbooks are in upright quarto format, and each contains a title page, dedication, twenty-one numbered pages of music, and a table of contents.[14] The *partitura* is an oblong quarto in *a libro aperto* format, in which the four-staff systems run from the left margin of the *verso* directly across the binding to the right margin of the facing *recto*. There are two systems per page throughout. Barring is every breve in duple meter and every three or six breves in triple meter, with few exceptions. The volume consists of a title page [no dedication], ninety-one pages of music, numbered 1–69, 80–101 [no pages 70–79], and a table of contents.

The printing of a full-score accompanimental *partitura* for keyboard along with the four partbooks is characteristic of publications by Milanese printers in the first part of the seventeenth century,[15] and represents an ideal for accompaniment appropriately expressed by Domenico Rognoni Taeggio: "some friends have told me that these works would ordinarily be played, and that a *partito* is required; thus to satisfy them I published it, knowing that in any case the full score is better than basso continuo."[16] There was considerable disagreement among musicians regarding accompanimental procedure at the onset of the basso continuo period; Cangiasi follows the Milanese tradition in this respect, implicitly favoring strict accompanimental doubling of the instrumental parts.[17]

The partbooks and *partitura* have equal claim to authority; editorial policy with regard to variants between the two has been to follow the preferable source when there are clear errors in one or the other (e.g., no. 4, *alto* and *tenore*, m. 33); to employ accidentals found in either source if there is ambiguity (e.g., no. 12, *canto*, m. 13); to leave accidentals as they stand in the *partitura* if there is no ambiguity regarding *musica ficta* (e.g., no. 3, *alto*, m. 44); and to follow the *partitura* reading in non-significant variants (e.g., no. 4, *alto*, mm. 35 and 37). All variants are reported below. Part designations for all pieces, lacking in the *partitura*, are taken from the partbooks. Final longs and maximas in the source appear as breves, dotted breves, or semibreves with fermatas, in accordance with modern convention. Original barring of the *partitura* is retained in this edition, with the exception of added barlines before the final notes of nos. 2, 6, 9, and 18.

Spelling, capitalization, and punctuation of the titles and dedications of the pieces follow the form given in the *partitura* unless noted otherwise below. The partbook dedications regularly abbreviate words in different ways than the *partitura*. Minor differences in orthography and punctuation in the titles and dedications are not reported here. One ligature is found in the source:

9. Canzon nona, basso, m. 29 (two semibreves).

Coloration occurs in the following triple-meter passages:

8. Canzon ottava:
    M. 51, alto and basso, notes 4 and 5 (partitura only).
    M. 51, tenore, notes 3 and 4 (partitura only).
    M. 60, alto, tenore, and basso (partitura only).

13. Canzon decimaterza:
    M. 57, canto, notes 3 and 4 (partitura only).
    M. 57, alto, notes 4 and 5 (partitura only).
    M. 59, basso, notes 6 and 7 (partitura only).

16. Canzon decimasesta:
    Mm. 48–51, canto, alto, tenore, and basso.

20. Canzon vigesima:
    M. 62, basso, notes 6 and 7.
    M. 65, alto, notes 6 and 7.

The combinations of clefs in the original are:

G2, C1, C3, F3: 11
G2, C2, C3, F3: 3, 4, 5, 8, 14, 17, 19, 20
C1, C2, C3, F4: 10
C1, C2, C4, F4: 1, 2, 6, 7, 12, 16
C1, C3, C4, F3: 13
C1, C3, C4, F4: 9, 15, 18, 21

The following variants, mistakes, and omissions in the sources may be noted:

1. Canzon prima, L'Obligata:
    Alto, m. 5, last note, the sharp is lacking in the partbook.
    Tenore, m. 35, note 1 is an *f* in the partitura.
    Alto, m. 35, note 4 is a *g'* in the partitura.
    Alto, m. 43, last note, the sharp is lacking in the partitura.
    Basso, m. 44, note 2 is an *e* in the partitura.
    Canto, m. 45, last note, the sharp is lacking in the partbook.
    Tenore, m. 51, note 2 is an *a* in the partitura (cf. m. 43).
    Canto, m. 55, note 2, the sharp is lacking in the partbook.
    Alto, m. 55, notes 1 and 2 are *f' f'* in the partitura.

2. Canzon seconda, La Consigliata:
    Alto, m. 31, the last note is a *d'* in the partitura.
    Canto, m. 46, the partitura notes are *g'* semiminim, *a'* minim, *g'* semibreve, *f'*# minim.
    Tenore, m. 47, the note is a *g* in the partitura.

3. Canzon terza, La Marina:
   Alto, m. 44, there is an extraneous *g'* semiminim before note 1 in the partitura.
   Alto, m. 44, notes 2 and 3 both have flats in the partbook.
   Tenore, m. 55, the note is a *d'* in the partitura.

4. Canzon quarta, La Marina:
   Canto, mm. 21–22, the tie is lacking in the partbook.
   Basso, m. 22, notes 1 and 4 both have flats in the partbook.
   Tenore, m. 25, note 3 is a *b*-flat in the partitura.
   Canto, m. 27, notes 6 and 7 both have sharps in the partbook.
   Canto, m. 28, notes 7 and 8 both have sharps in the partbook.
   Alto, m. 30, note 3 is lacking in the partbook.
   Canto, m. 33, note 4, the sharp is lacking in the partbook.
   Alto and tenore, m. 33, the parts are reversed in the partitura; notes intended for the alto are placed in the tenore, and vice versa.
   Alto, m. 34, note 1 is a *g'* in the partitura.
   Tenore, m. 34, note 1 is a *d'* in the partitura.
   Alto, m. 35, notes 3–6 are replaced by three minims *b'*-flat, *f'*, *a'* in the partbook.
   Alto, m. 37, notes 1–3 are replaced by a *b'*-flat dotted minim and three semiminims *f'*, *a'*, *a'* in the partbook.
   Canto, m. 38, notes 9–12 are replaced by a *g"* minim in the partitura.
   Tenore, m. 38, the dotted minim is replaced by a minim and semiminim in the partbook.
   Canto, m. 39, note 1 is replaced by two *c"* semiminims in the partitura.
   Canto, m. 39, the last note has a sharp in the partbook.
   Alto, m. 42, the last note is an *e'* in the partitura.
   Tenore, m. 42, note 1 is an *f'* in the partitura.
   Tenore, m. 46, the note is a *g* in the partbook.

5. Canzon quinta, La Stella:
   Tenore, m. 6, note 4 is replaced by two semiminims in the partbook.
   Tenore, m. 8, note 2, the sharp is lacking in the partitura.
   Canto, m. 9, note 3, the sharp is lacking in the partbook.
   Basso, m. 12, note 10, the flat is lacking in the partbook.
   Canto, m. 17, note 4 is replaced by two semiminims in the partbook.
   Canto, m. 23, notes 3 and 4 are lacking in the partbook.
   Canto, m. 26, note 3, the sharp is lacking in the partitura.
   Canto, m. 40, the semiminim rest is replaced by a *d"* in the partbook.

6. Canzon sesta, La Bussola:
   Alto, m. 12, notes 2 and 3 are *b'*, *a'* in the partitura.
   Alto, m. 14, the last note is a *g* in the partitura.
   Alto, m. 26, last note, the flat is lacking in the partbook.
   Canto, m. 43, notes 3 and 5, the sharps are lacking in the partitura.
   Canto, m. 45, note 5, the flat is lacking in the partitura.

7. Canzon settima, La Grassa:
   Canto, m. 9, note 2 is a *c"* in the partbook (cf. m. 16).
   Tenore, m. 17, note 1 is a semiminim in the partitura.
   Alto, m. 19, note 1 is lacking in the partbook.
   Tenore, m. 20, note 2, the sharp is lacking in the partitura.
   Basso, m. 20, note 1 is an *f* in the partitura.
   Alto, m. 21, notes 2–3, the sharps are lacking in the partitura.
   Alto, m. 25, note 4 is an *f'* in the partitura.

Basso, m. 27, notes 2–3 and 7–8 are an octave higher in the partitura.
Alto, m. 30, notes 5 and 6 are replaced by two *g'* minims in the partitura.
Basso, m. 33, notes 4–7 are an octave higher in the partitura.
Basso, m. 34, notes 3, 4, and 6 are an octave higher in the partitura.
Canto, m. 36, note 5 is an *a'* in the partbook.
Alto, m. 44, note 3 is an *f'* in the partbook.
Tenore, m. 48, the last note is a *g* in the partbook.

8. Canzon ottava, La Grassa:
Basso, m. 27, note 1 is an *f* in the partitura.
Basso, m. 30, note 2, the flat is lacking in the partitura.
Canto, m. 35, the note is replaced by a rest in the partitura.
Tenore, m. 44, note 6 is a *b* in the partbook.

9. Canzon nona, La Theorica:
The dedication in the partitura is lacking after the word "Lettore."
Canto, m. 7, note 5, the sharp is lacking in the partitura.
Alto, m. 10, notes 5 and 7, the sharps are lacking in the partitura.
Alto, m. 11, note 2, the sharp is lacking in the partitura.
Tenore, m. 19, notes 1 and 2 are *d'* and *c'*, respectively, in the partitura.
Canto, m. 22, note 2, the sharp is lacking in the partitura.
Basso, m. 25, note 9, the flat is lacking in the partitura.
Basso, m. 26, last note, the flat is lacking in the partbook.
Alto, m. 33, notes 5 and 6 are replaced by an *e'* semiminim and *d'*, *c'* fusae in the partitura.
Alto, m. 48, notes 7 and 8 are *a* and *c'*, respectively, in the partitura.
Alto, m. 51, the sharp is lacking in the partitura.

10. Canzon decima, La Guerra:
Tenore, m. 1, the clef is C3 in the partitura.
Alto, m. 5, notes 2 and 3, the sharps are lacking in the partbook.
Alto, m. 5, notes 4 and 5, both notes have sharps in the partbook.
Alto, m. 6, note 1, the sharp is lacking in the partitura.
Tenore, m. 6, the last note is a *c'* in the partitura.
Canto, m. 7, last note, the sharp is lacking in the partbook.
Canto, m. 9, note 3 is a semiminim in the partitura.
Alto, m. 12, notes 2 and 3, the sharps are lacking in the partbook.
Alto, m. 12, notes 4 and 5, both notes have sharps in the partbook.
Alto, m. 13, note 1, the sharp is lacking in the partitura.
Canto, m. 14, last note, the sharp is lacking in the partbook.
Alto, m. 20, note 4 is an *e'* in the partitura.
Alto, m. 23, note 4 is a *d'* in the partitura.
Alto, m. 23, note 8 is a *d'* in the partitura.
Canto, m. 37, note 3, the sharp is lacking in the partbook.
Alto, m. 38, there is an extraneous *e'* minim between notes 1 and 2 in the partbook.
Alto, m. 39, note 4 is an *e'* in the partitura (cf. m. 20).
Alto, m. 42, note 4 is a *d'* in the partitura (cf. m. 23).
Canto, m. 43, note 3, the sharp is lacking in the partitura.
Alto, m. 47, note 5 is a *d'* in the partitura.
Alto, m. 53, the last note is an *f'* in the partitura.
Alto, m. 54, last note, the sharp is lacking in the partbook.

Alto, m. 56, note 3, the sharp is lacking in the partbook.

11. Canzon undecima, La Capitania:
    Alto, m. 5, note 3, the sharp is lacking in the partitura.
    Tenore, m. 9, note 10 is an *f'* in the partitura.
    Tenore, m. 13, note 1 is a *d'* in the partitura (cf. m. 28).
    Canto, m. 21, note 3 is a minim in the partitura.
    Alto, m. 21, note 5 is a dotted minim in the partitura.
    Alto, m. 33, note 6 is a *d'* in the partitura.
    Alto, m. 45, note 3, the sharp is lacking in the partbook.
    Canto, m. 61, note 6 is lacking in the partbook.
    Tenore, m. 62, note 4 is a fusa in the partitura.

12. Canzon duodecima, La Bassa:
    Alto, m. 2, note 1, the natural sign is lacking in the partitura.
    Tenore, m. 5, notes 1 and 2 are lacking the sharp and natural sign, respectively, in the partbook.
    Alto and tenore, m. 6, beats 3 and 4, the parts are reversed in the partitura; the rest and note intended for the tenore are placed in the alto, and the rest intended for the alto is placed in the tenore.
    Basso, m. 6, note 7, the sharp is lacking in the partitura.
    Canto, m. 8, note 2, the sharp is lacking in the partitura.
    Canto, m. 13, note 12, the flat is lacking in the partitura.
    Basso, m. 18, the last note is a *B*-natural in the partbook.
    Tenore, m. 27, note 9, the sharp is lacking in the partbook.
    Alto, m. 33, note 6 is a *d'* in the partitura.
    Canto, m. 40, note 10, the sharp is lacking in the partbook.
    Basso, m. 40, note 2 is a *c* in the partitura.
    Alto, m. 45, notes 13 and 16 have sharps in the partbook.
    Alto, m. 57, notes 1 and 2, the sharps are lacking in the partbook.

13. Canzon decimaterza, La Torta:
    Tenore, m. 4, note 2 is a semiminim in the partitura.
    Canto, m. 6, last note, the sharp is lacking in the partbook.
    Canto, m. 12, note 1 is a *b'* in the partitura.
    Tenore, m. 16, note 2, the sharp is lacking in the partitura.
    Tenore, m. 32, note 2, the sharp is lacking in the partitura.
    Basso, m. 34, notes 1 and 2 have cautionary natural signs in the partbook.
    Canto, m. 52, last note, the sharp is lacking in the partbook.
    Canto, m. 57, note 1, the sharp is lacking in the partitura.
    Canto, m. 58, note 1 is a *b'* in the partitura.
    Canto, m. 58, notes 4–6 are repeated extraneously in the partbook.
    Basso, m. 61, notes 2 and 3 are an octave higher in the partitura.
    Tenore, m. 62, note 2 is a *g* in the partitura.
    Basso, m. 62, the note is an octave higher in the partitura.

14. Canzon decimaquarta, La Filippa:
    Basso, m. 4, the last note has a sharp in the partbook.
    Alto, m. 8, the sharp is placed between notes 4 and 5 in the partbook.
    Basso, mm. 11–12, the tie is lacking in the partitura.
    Tenore, m. 18, the breve is replaced by two semibreves in the partitura.

Tenore, m. 27, the rest is replaced by two *b* minims and an *a* semibreve in the partitura.
Alto, m. 34, note 3, the sharp is lacking in the partbook.
Canto, m. 37, note 3, the sharp is lacking in the partbook.
Alto, mm. 54–55, the tie is lacking in the partbook.
Canto, m. 55, note 3, the natural sign is lacking in the partbook.
Alto, mm. 55–56, the breve and semibreve are replaced by a dotted breve in the partbook.
Canto, mm. 58–59, the minim tied to a semiminim and followed by two fusae is replaced by a *g'* semibreve in the partbook.
Alto, m. 61, the sharp is placed between notes 6 and 7 in the partbook.
Alto, m. 63, the sharp is placed between notes 6 and 7 in the partbook.

15. Canzon decimaquinta, La Fiorina:
Alto, m. 7, note 5 is a *g* in the partbook.
Canto, m. 8, notes 3 and 4 are replaced by *e'* and *g'* minims in the partitura.
Alto, m. 17, note 7, the sharp is lacking in the partitura.
Tenore, m. 19, there is an extraneous *g* semiminim after the last note in the partitura.
Alto, m. 20, notes 3 and 4 are lacking in the partbook.
Tenore, m. 31, the last note is a *d* in the partbook.
Alto, m. 33, note 6 is an *e'* in the partitura.
Tenore, m. 34, notes 1–3 are replaced by a *d'* minim in the partbook.
Basso, m. 37, note 5, the sharp is lacking in the partitura.
Canto, m. 59, the last note has a sharp in the partbook.

16. Canzon decimasesta, La Girometta:
Basso, m. 14, notes 3 and 4 are fusae in the partbook.
Alto, m. 15, note 2 is a *c'* in the partitura.
Tenore, m. 29, note 2 is a *b* in the partitura.
Canto, m. 35, the last note has a sharp in the partbook.
Alto, m. 39, notes 1, 2, 3, and 5 have sharps in the partbook.
Alto, m. 40, notes 1, 2, 3, 5, 6, 7, and 8 have sharps in the partbook.
Canto, m. 41, note 5, the sharp is lacking in the partitura.
Canto, m. 46, note 5, the sharp is lacking in the partitura.
Alto, m. 54, the last note is an *a'* in the partitura.

17. Canzon decimasettima, La Genovesa:
Alto, m. 11, note 4 has a sharp in the partbook.
Alto, m. 28, note 4 has a sharp in the partbook.
Tenore, m. 32, notes 5–8 are replaced by two *b* minims in the partitura.
Tenore, m. 34, the last note is a semiminim in the partitura.
Basso, m. 35, the last note has a flat in the partbook.
Tenore, m. 43, the semibreve rest is lacking in the partbook.
Canto, m. 46, last note, the sharp is lacking in the partbook.
Canto, m. 47, notes 6–10 are lacking in the partbook.
Alto, m. 49, note 6, the sharp is lacking in the partbook.
Tenore, m. 59, the last note has a sharp in the partbook.
Alto, m. 65, notes 1 and 5, the sharps are lacking in the partitura.

18. Canzon decimaottava, La Alessandrina:
Canto, m. 15, the last note is an *f'* in the partitura.
Canto, mm. 20–21, the semibreve tied to breve is replaced by a breve (dot lacking) in the partitura.
Alto, m. 29, note 1 is a semiminim in the partitura.
Tenore, m. 30, the last note has a sharp in the partbook.
Alto, m. 39, note 2, the sharp is lacking in the partitura.
Alto, mm. 53–54, the tie is lacking in the partitura.
Basso, m. 54, notes 1 and 2 are replaced by an *e* minim in the partbook.
Alto, m. 58, note 3 is an *e'* in the partitura.
Basso, m. 58, the rest is the value of a breve in the partbook.

19. Canzon decimanona, La Confrata:
Basso, m. 44, note 1 is a semiminim in the partitura.
Basso, m. 44, note 2 is an *e* in the partitura.
Canto, m. 54, note 4 is a semiminim in the partitura.

20. Canzon vigesima, La Furugada:
Basso, m. 2, the last note is a *d* in the partitura.
Basso, m. 23, note 2 is replaced by two minims in the partbook.
Alto, mm. 23–24, the tied breve and semibreve are replaced by a semibreve and two tied semibreves in the partitura.
Basso, m. 24, there is an extraneous *a* semibreve after the last note in the partitura.
Tenore, m. 33, notes 2, 4, 5, 7, 9, and 10 have sharps in the partbook.
Canto, m. 34, the last note is replaced by two *e'* semiminims in the partbook.

Tenore, m. 34, notes 2, 4, and 5 have sharps in the partbook.
Canto, m. 36, note 4 is replaced by two *b* semiminims in the partbook.
Tenore, m. 37, there is an extraneous *c'* minim between notes 2 and 3 in the partitura.
Alto, m. 39, there is an extraneous *a'* fusa between notes 5 and 6 in the partitura.
Alto, mm. 40–41, the three semibreves are replaced by a dotted breve in the partbook.
Canto, m. 47, notes 1 and 2 are *e"* and *c"*, respectively, in the partitura.
Alto, m. 48, the last note is replaced by two *a'* semiminims in the partbook.
Tenore, m. 49, notes 5 and 6 are *d'* and *e'*, respectively.
Tenore, m. 50, notes 1 and 2 are *f'* and *d'*, respectively.
Tenore, m. 54, note 1 is an *e'* in the partitura.
Basso, m. 54, notes 5 and 6 are replaced by a semiminim in the partbook.
Basso, m. 56, note 6 has a flat in the partbook.
Alto, m. 58, the last note is an *f'* in the partitura.
Tenore, m. 58, notes 1–3 are fusa, fusa, semiminim in the partitura.
Alto, m. 59, note 3 has a sharp in the partbook.
Alto, m. 64, note 6, the flat is lacking in the partitura.
M. 67 is repeated in the partitura.
Tenore, m. 70, the last note is a *c'* in the partitura.

21. Canzon vigesimaprima, La Pessa:
Alto, m. 7, last note, the sharp is lacking in the partbook.
Alto, m. 19, note 2, the sharp is lacking in the partitura.
Alto, m. 21, the last note is a *d'* in the partitura.
Canto, m. 29, note 2 is a *b'* in the partitura.
Alto, m. 50, note 4 is a *d'* in the partitura.

NOTES

1. Oscar Mischiati, "Cangiasi, Giovanni Antonio," *Die Musik in Geschichte und Gegenwart*, ed. Friedrich Blume (Kassel, 1973), XV, 1290–91. The unsigned "Cangiasi, Giovanni Antonio," *The New Grove Dictionary of Music and Musicians*, ed. Stanley Sadie (20 vols., London, 1980), III, 683–84, appears to be based on Mischiati's work, but contains a number of inaccuracies and discrepancies.

2. Robert Eitner, *Biographisch-bibliographische Quellen-Lexicon der Musiker und Musikgelehrten* (10 vols., Leipzig, 1898–1904), II, 306.

3. *Lista delli libri fatti stampare dalli heredi di Francesco & Simon librari in Milano* [1596]. See Mischiati, *Indici, cataloghi e avvisi degli editori e librai musicali italiani dal 1591 al 1798* (Florence, 1982), p. 109. The eleven four-voice madrigals found in MS Turin, Biblioteca Nazionale, raccolta Foà 4 almost certainly originated in this volume. See Mischiati, "L'intavolatura d'organo tedesca della Biblioteca Nazionale di Torino: catalogo ragionato," *L'Organo*, 4 (1963), 88.

4. Other noteworthy organists who published little or no keyboard music include Ascanio, Bariolla, Luzzaschi, Milleville, Pallavicino, E. Pasquini, and Stivori. See Robert Judd, "The Use of Notational Formats at the Keyboard" (D. Phil. dissertation, Oxford University, 1989), I, 107.

5. See Wolfram Steinbeck, "Scherzo," *Handwörterbuch der musikalischen Terminologie*, ed. Hans Heinrich Eggebrecht (Wiesbaden, 1985). The first musical reference to *scherzo* is Monteverdi's *Scherzi musicali* (Venice, 1607), which had been written by the end of the previous century; Cangiasi's works bear no relation to either the vocal music or instrumental ritornelli of Monteverdi's *Scherzi*. Cangiasi's choice of title is reminiscent of other somewhat fanciful titles of the period: Bariolla's *Capricci* (1594; see Volume 12 of the present Series), Negri's *Affetti* (1611d), and Ercole Porta's *Vaga ghirlanda di soavi et odorati fiori musicali* (1613c), to name a few. (Dates followed by a lower-case letter refer to the listings of the works in Claudio Sartori, *Bibliografia della musica strumentale italiana stampata in Italia fino al 1700* [2 vols., Florence, 1952 and 1968]).

6. Castelnuovo di Scrivia has an extensive entry in Leandro Alberti's *Descrittione di Tutta Italia* (Venice, 1558), f. 369, in which the ancient fortification (dating from the time of the invasion of the Goths) and its surroundings are described.

7. See Sartori, "Une pratique des musiciens lombards (1582–1639), l'hommage des chansons instrumentales aux familles d'une ville," *La musique instrumentale de la renaissance*, ed. Jean Jacquot (Paris, 1955), pp. 305–12.

8. In which case the title would place the work in Sartori's class of works whose titles reflect their spirit. See Sartori, "Une pratique," p. 307.

9. The most important volumes of the line are published in the present series, which extends from the first collection of instrumental canzonas, Florentio Maschera's 1582 volume, to Giacomo Filippo Biumi's volume of 1627. While a full survey of the canzona literature has yet to be undertaken, the first part of the repertoire has been examined in Dietrich Kämper, *Studien zur instrumentalen Ensemblemusik des 16. Jahrhunderts in Italien* (Cologne, 1970), pp. 192–232.

10. For volumes that contain accompanimental parts prior to Viadana, see Otto Kinkeldey, *Orgel und Klavier in der Musik des 16. Jahrhunderts* (Leipzig, 1910), pp. 192, 197–202. See also Imogene Horsley, "Full and Short Scores in the Accompaniment of Italian Church Music in the Early Baroque," *Journal of the American Musicological Society*, 30 (1977), 466–99.

11. See James Ladewig, "The Origins of Frescobaldi's Variation Canzonas Reappraised," *Frescobaldi Studies*, Sources of Music and Their Interpretation, vol. 1, ed. Alexander Silbiger (Durham, 1987), pp. 237–44.

12. This is an unusually early use of the descending chromatic subject later to occur so frequently. See Alan Curtis, *Sweelinck's Keyboard Music* (Leiden and London, 1972), p. 138.

13. Mischiati, "Cangiasi." Regarding the "Girometta" tune, see Warren Kirkendale, "Franceschina, Girometta, and their Companions in a Madrigal 'a diversi linguaggi' by Luca Marenzio and Orazio Vecchi," *Acta Musicologica*, 44 (1972), 196–98. This setting uses the major mode of the tune, unlike Floriano Canale's setting of 1600 (see Volume 14 of the present series, pp. xiii and 97). Kirkendale noted the relation between Cangiasi's setting and that of Giovanni Battista Fasolo's *Annuale* (Venice, 1645), ed. Rudolf Walter (Heidelberg, 1977), II, 87. The first four measures of the works are nearly identical, Fasolo proceeding in a quite different way (more oriented to a keyboard style) thereafter.

14. The tables of contents of the four partbooks (which are identical) do not accord with the actual contents (cf. Sartori, *Bibliografia*, 1614h); the *partitura* table of contents is correct.

15. See Judd, "Notational Formats," I, 113–16 for a summary of Milanese and Italian trends in printing according to city of publication.

16. "Mà alcuni amici m'hanno detto che questa opera ordinariamente sarà suonata, et che vi fà bisogno del Partito, onde per compiacerli l'ho dato fuori, conoscendo che in ogni caso meglio è il Partito, che il Basso continuato . . ." Rognoni Taeggio, *Canzoni à 4 & 8 voci* (Milan, 1605), as quoted in Sartori, *Bibliografia*, 1605a. See Volume 16 of the present series.

17. The debate is summarized in Judd, "Notational Formats," I, 129–32; for a detailed account, see Kinkeldey, *Orgel und Klavier*, pp. 187–213; F. T. Arnold, *The Art of Accompaniment from a Thorough-bass* (New York, 1965), pp. 67–69, 80–81; and Horsley, "Full and Short Scores."

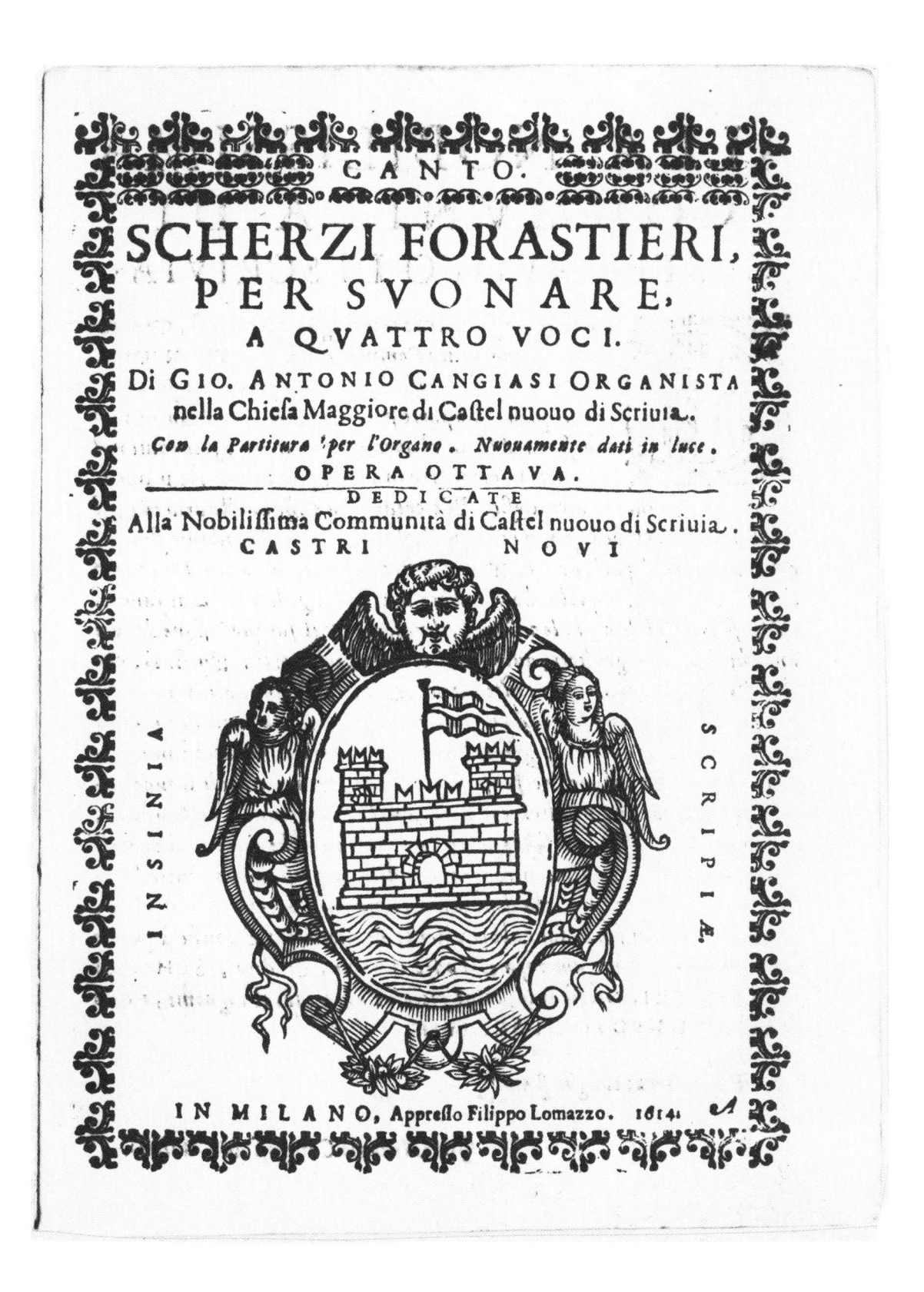

Plate 1. Title page from the *canto* partbook of Giovanni Antonio Cangiasi,
Scherzi forastieri per suonare a quattro voci (Milan, 1614)
(Reproduced by permission of the Biblioteca Capitolare, Verona)

ALLA NOBILISSIMA COMMVNITA DI CASTEL NVOVO DI SCRIVIA.

Li obligi infiniti, che teco tengo, ò Generosa, & non mai à pieno lodata Communità di CASTEL NVOVO, mi sforzano, s'io posso, à pagarli in parte con farti dono di questo mio parto partorito, e vero nel tuo amoroso seno: Mà da tè anco à dirne il vero fecondato nel concetto mio, mentre in questa patria tua sì caramente, & prontamente m'accogliesti. Ne creder' già, che questa aria tua, sì salubre, dolce, & benigna, ne che questo sito tuo tanto abbondante fertile, & ameno, per il quale ne sei, & con molta raggione da tante Terre, & Città inuidiata, sia quello che m'habbia allettato à godere de' tuoi fauori. Mà sì bene gli honori, le virtudi, il valore, & il sangue insigne de tuoi antichi illustri progenitori, quali sì al uiuo impressi porti. Questi sì, che sono stati quelli, quali come tante catene, & lacci m'hanno accinto, & legato di non potere, ne sapere da tè partirmi; & perciò da tante tue cortesie obligato pensai in questo tuo gentilissimo nido partorire, ne luoco à mio giuditio più atto, & insigne, ne persone più degne, & meriteuoli trouar poteuo per illustrare, & nobilitare il parto, qual in luce mando, ne solo è mio, ma tuo ancora, essendo insieme meco conceputo; poiche doue io suonando disponeuo l'essere, tù all'incontro, grata audienza prestandomi, introducesti la forma. Resta hora, che donato à tè, come tuo l'accetti, lo nutrischi, & alleui, & lo diffendi dal rabbioso dente de mordaci; E poiche à questo parto impongo, come amorosa Madre il nome, & dico, SCHERZI FORASTIERI, così tù anco, come pietoso Padre dalli il cognome, e dilli di CASTEL NVOVO DI SCRIVIA.

Vostro Seruo obligatissimo

Gio. Antonio Cangiasi da Milano.

Plate 2. Dedication page from the *canto* partbook of Giovanni Antonio Cangiasi,
Scherzi forastieri per suonare a quattro voci (Milan, 1614)
(Reproduced by permission of the Biblioteca Capitolare, Verona)

1. Canzon prima, L'Obligata

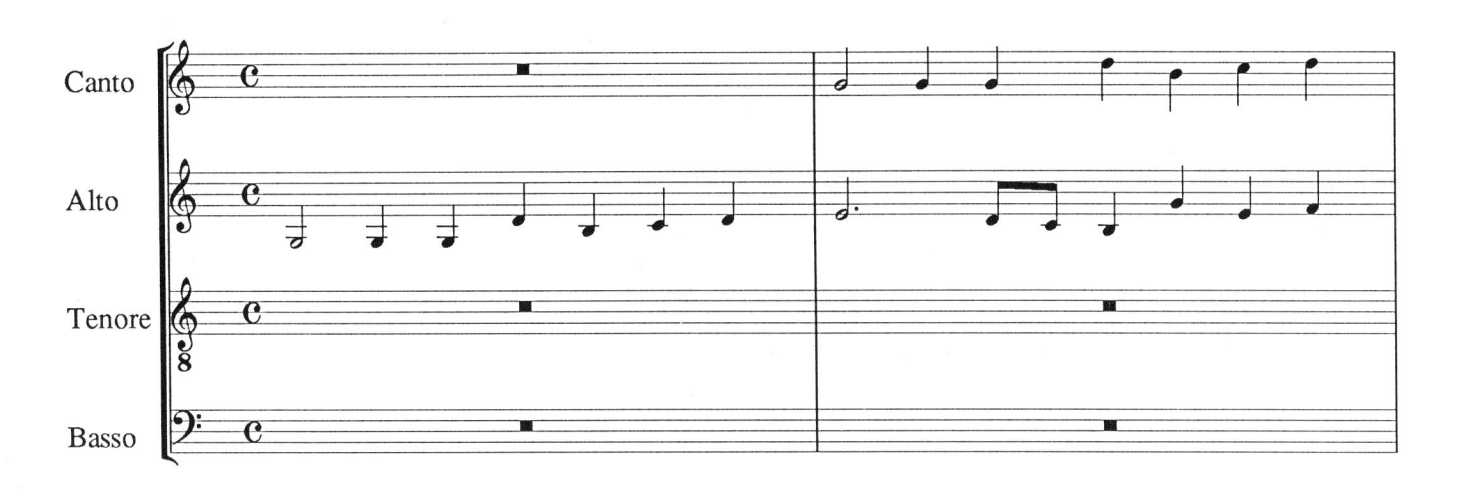

Canzon prima, L'Obligata

Canzon prima, L'Obligata

4   CANZON PRIMA, L'OBLIGATA

CANZON PRIMA, L'OBLIGATA   5

6 CANZON PRIMA, L'OBLIGATA

CANZON PRIMA, L'OBLIGATA 7

8 CANZON PRIMA, L'OBLIGATA

2. Canzon seconda, La Consigliata

Canzon seconda, La Consigliata

CANZON SECONDA, LA CONSIGLIATA

12 Canzon seconda, La Consigliata

CANZON SECONDA, LA CONSIGLIATA   13

14   Canzon seconda, La Consigliata

CANZON SECONDA, LA CONSIGLIATA 15

3. Canzon terza, La Marina

CANZON TERZA, LA MARINA 17

18   Canzon terza, La Marina

CANZON TERZA, LA MARINA 19

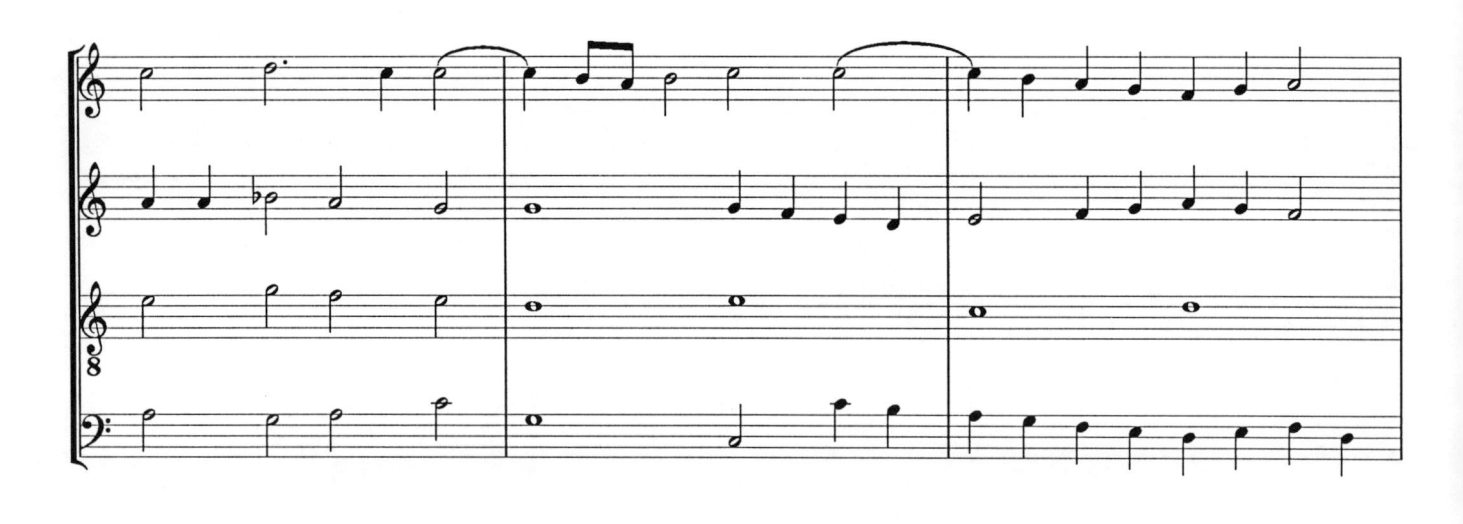

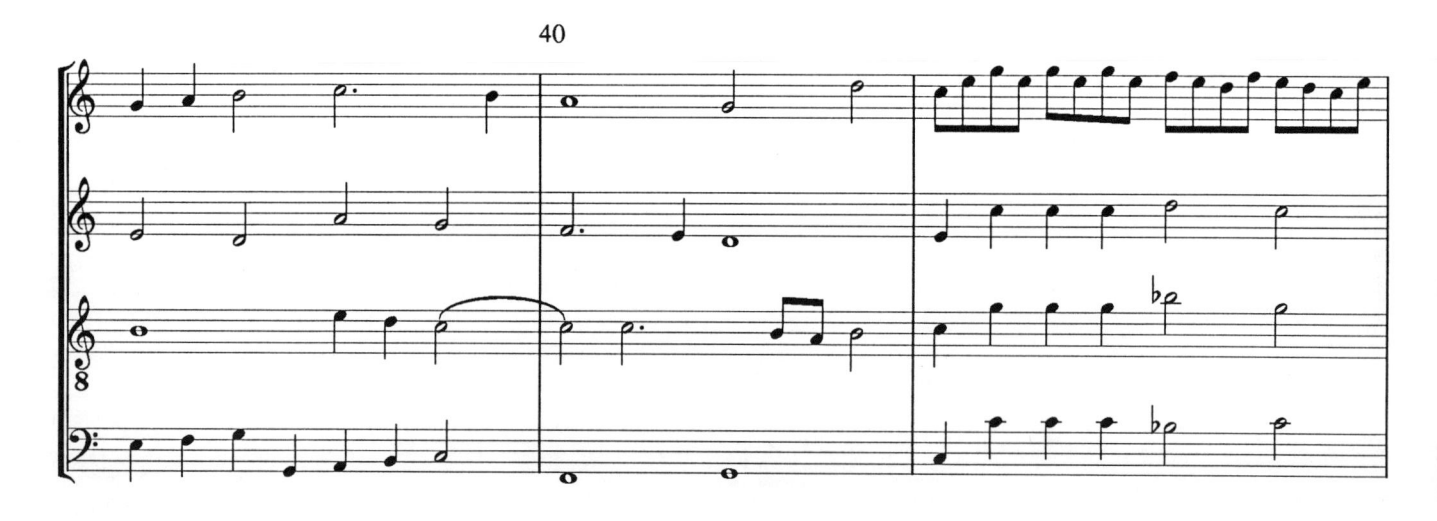

20 Canzon terza, La Marina

CANZON TERZA, LA MARINA 21

22 Canzon terza, La Marina

4. Canzon quarta, La Marina

24 CANZON QUARTA, LA MARINA

CANZON QUARTA, LA MARINA 25

26   Canzon quarta, La Marina

CANZON QUARTA, LA MARINA 27

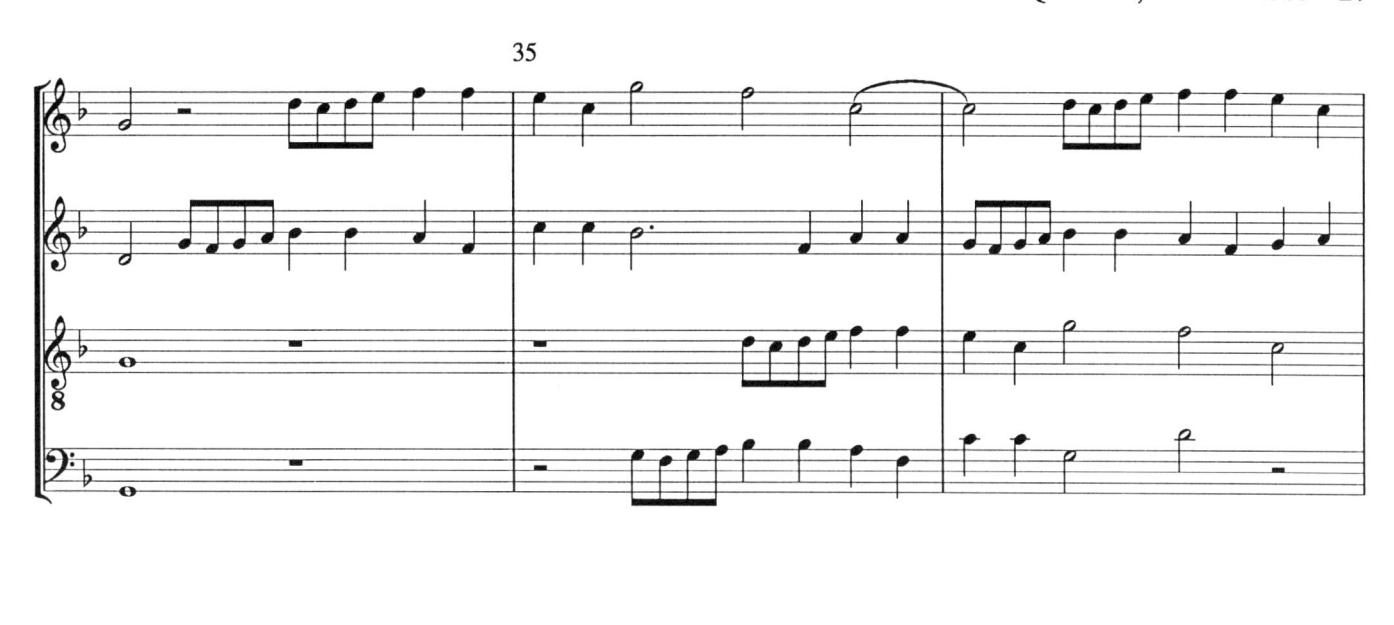

28 CANZON QUARTA, LA MARINA

5. Canzon quinta, La Stella

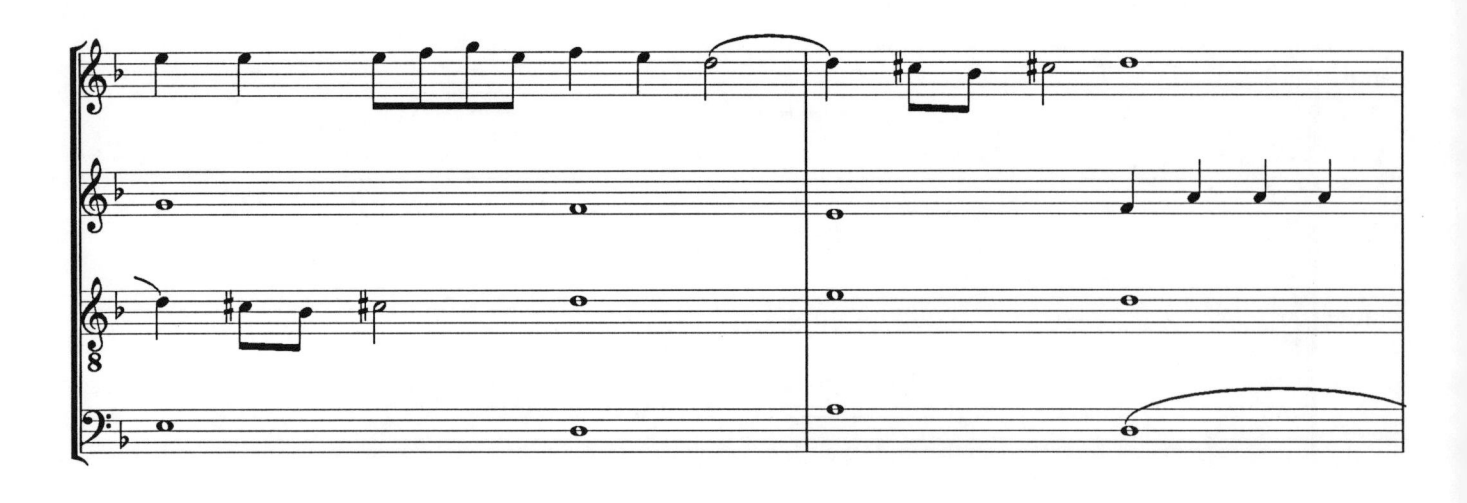

Canzon quinta, La Stella

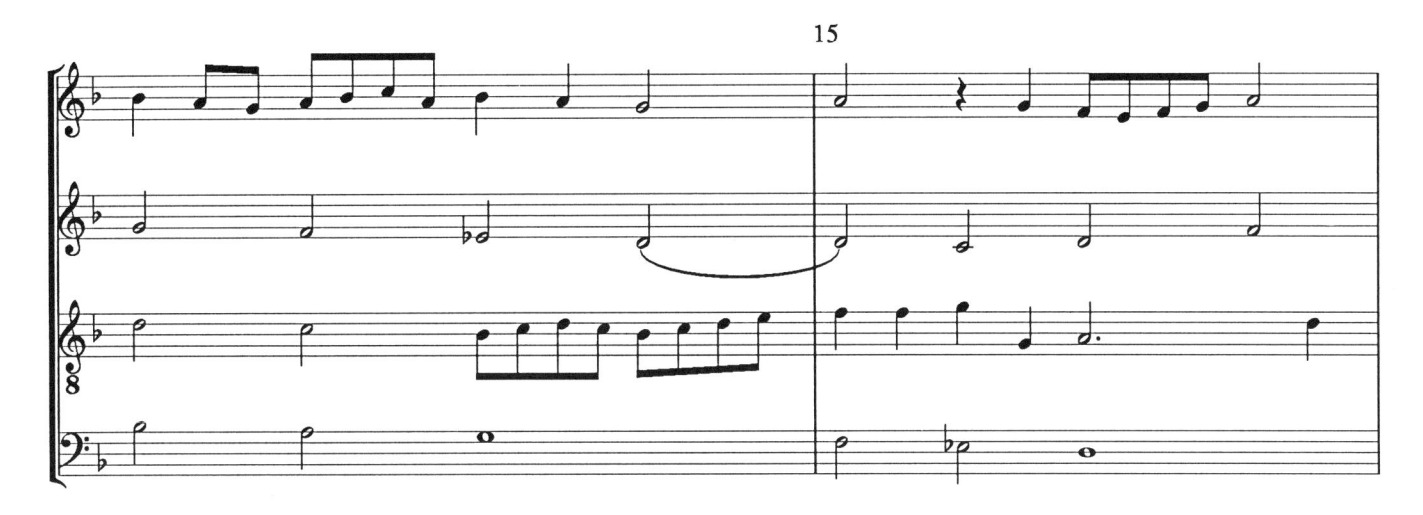

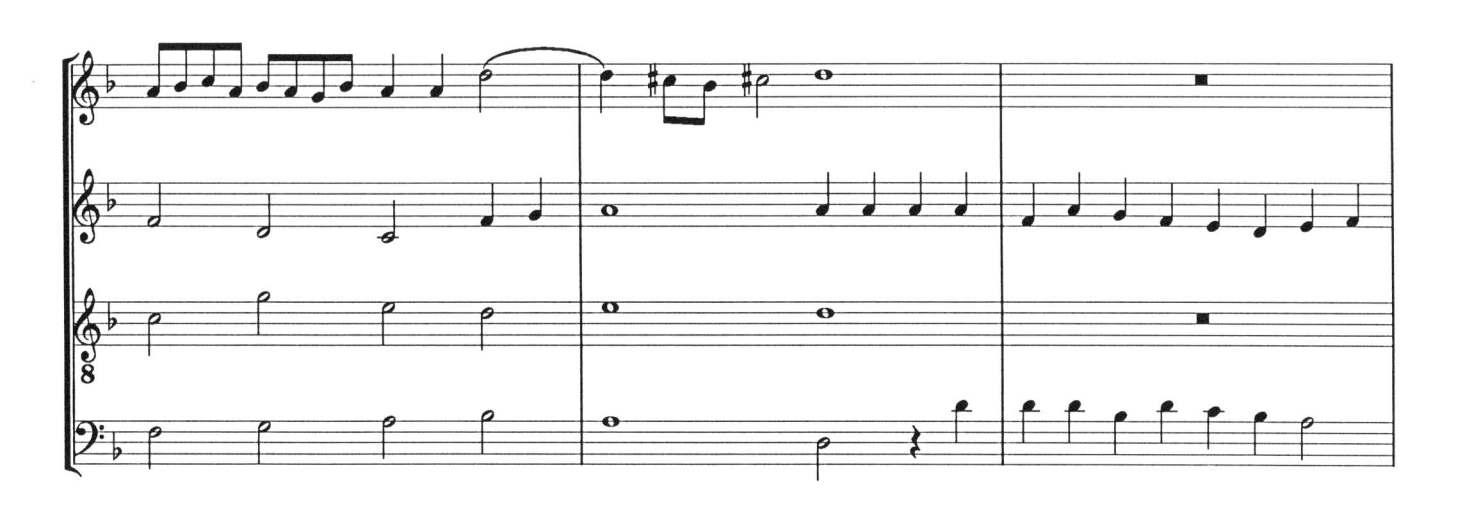

CANZON QUINTA, LA STELLA

32 Canzon quinta, La Stella

CANZON QUINTA, LA STELLA   33

Canzon quinta, La Stella

6. Canzon sesta, La Bussola

36 CANZON SESTA, LA BUSSOLA

CANZON SESTA, LA BUSSOLA 37

38 CANZON SESTA, LA BUSSOLA

CANZON SESTA, LA BUSSOLA 39

40 Canzon sesta, La Bussola

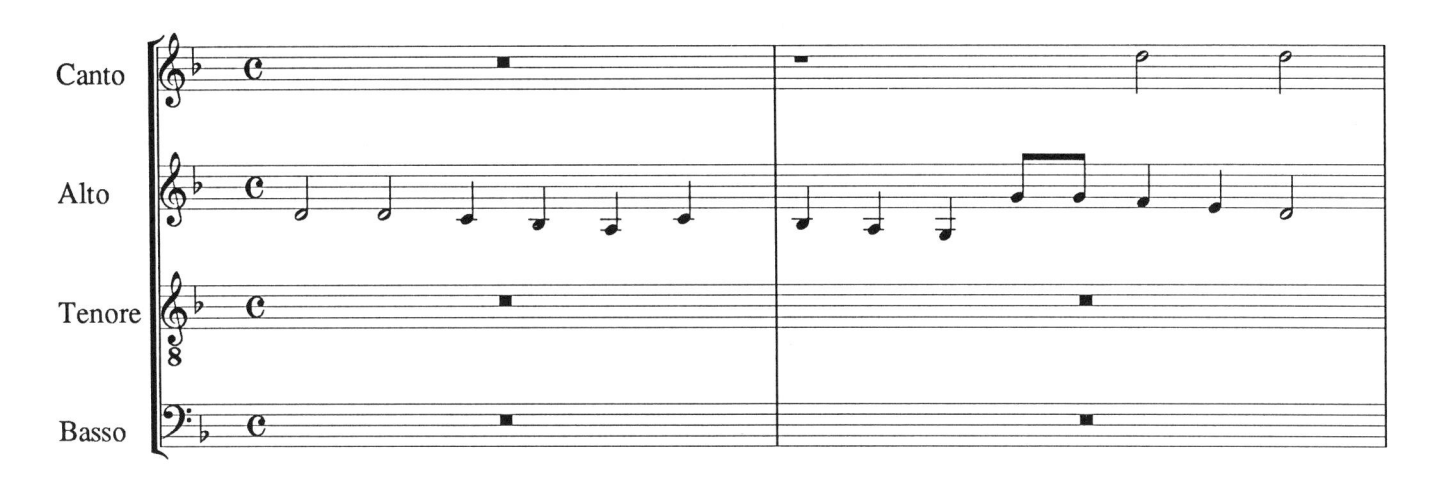

7. Canzon settima, La Grassa

42 CANZON SETTIMA, LA GRASSA

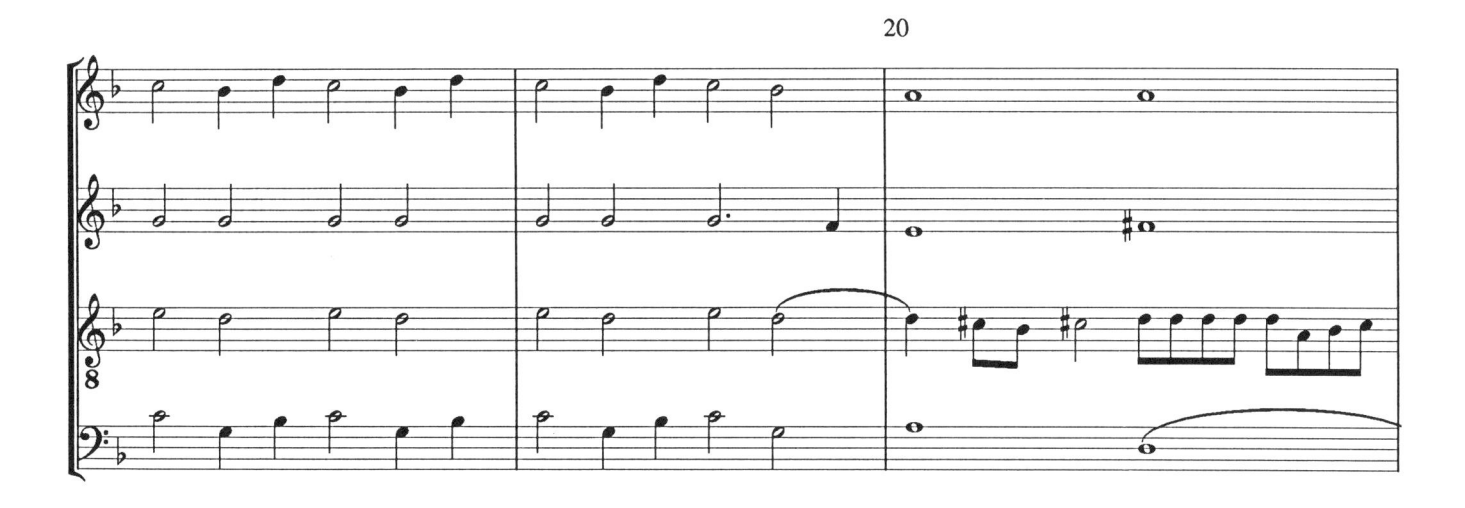

CANZON SETTIMA, LA GRASSA 43

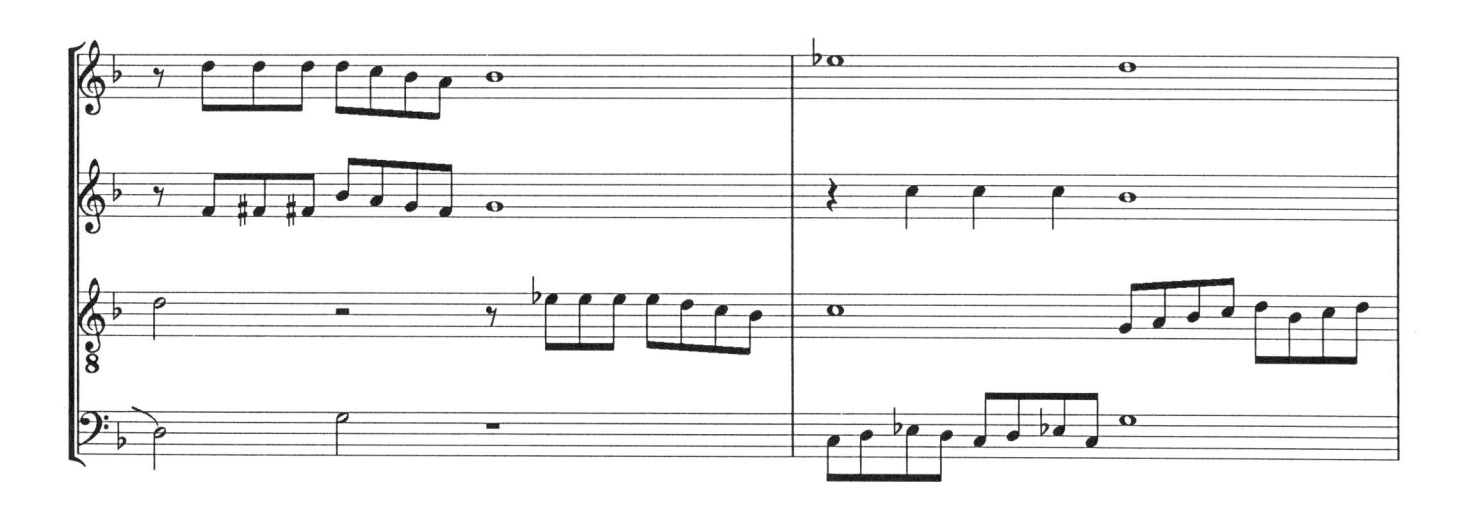

44   Canzon settima, La Grassa

CANZON SETTIMA, LA GRASSA   45

46   Canzon settima, La Grassa

CANZON SETTIMA, LA GRASSA   47

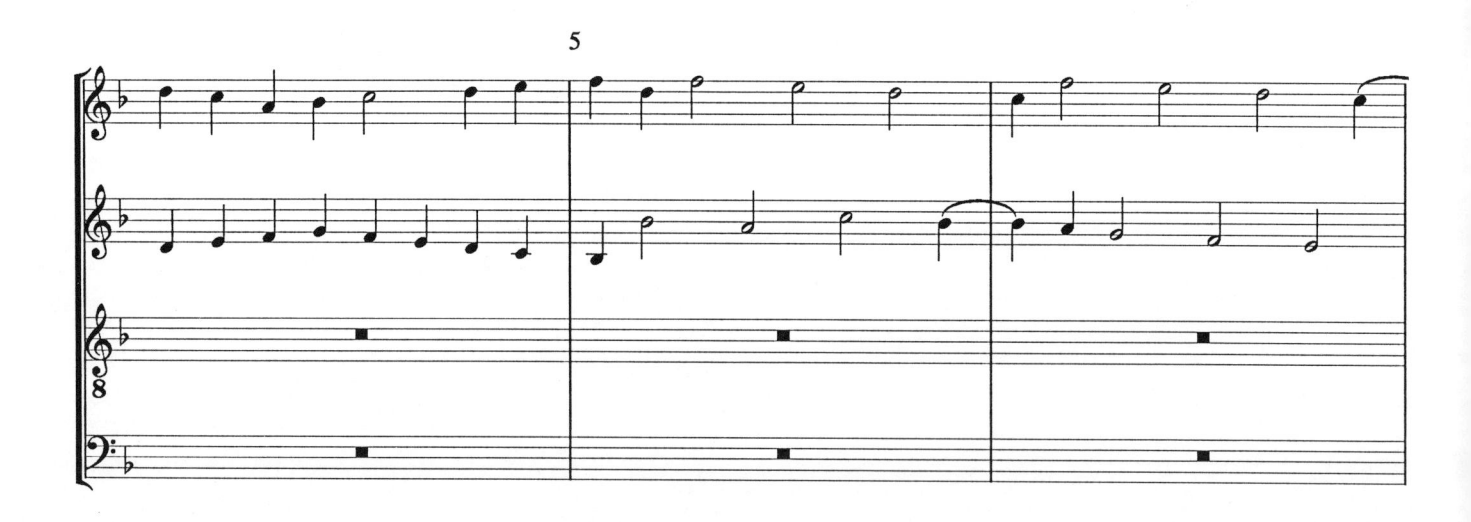

8. Canzon ottava, La Grassa

CANZON OTTAVA, LA GRASSA 49

50   Canzon ottava, La Grassa

CANZON OTTAVA, LA GRASSA 51

Canzon ottava, La Grassa

CANZON OTTAVA, LA GRASSA 53

54   Canzon ottava, La Grassa

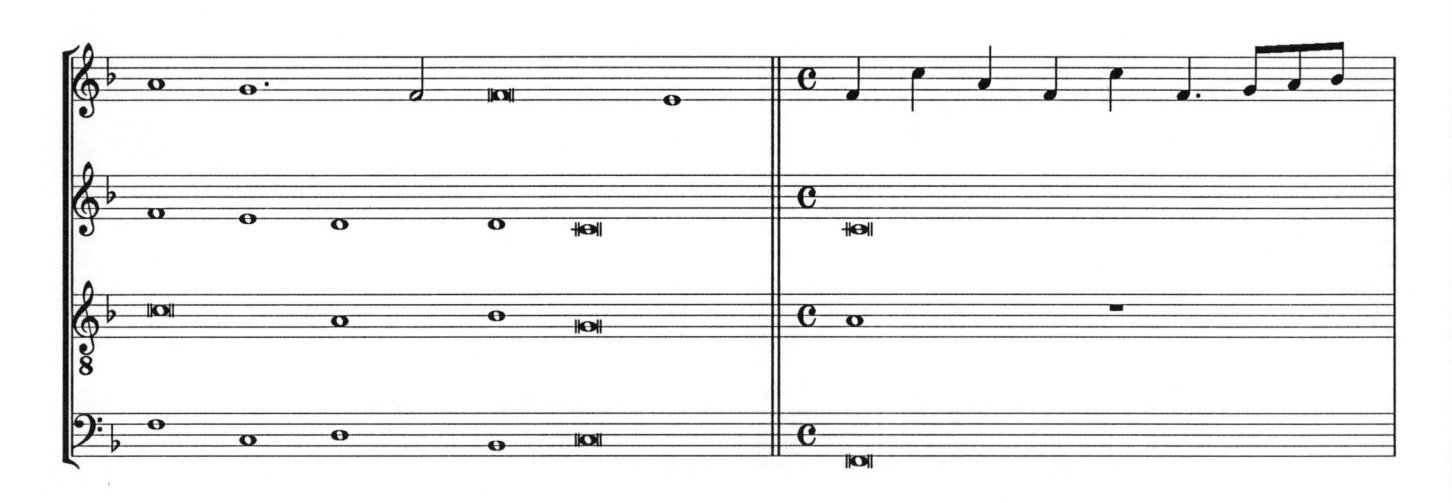

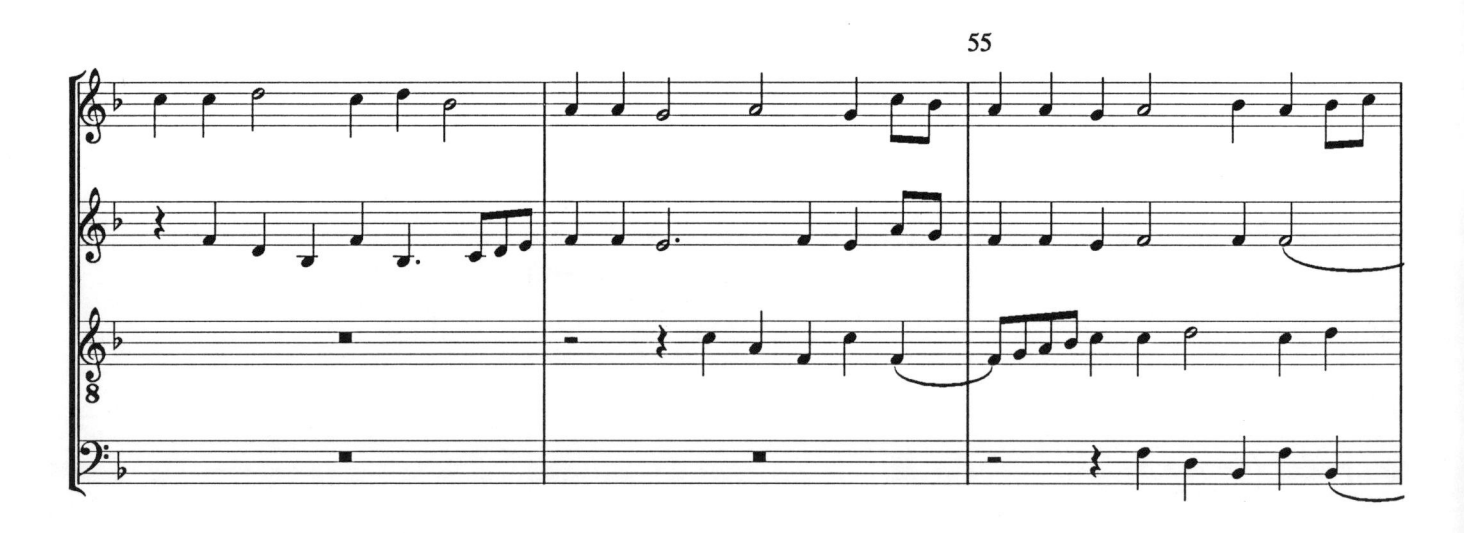

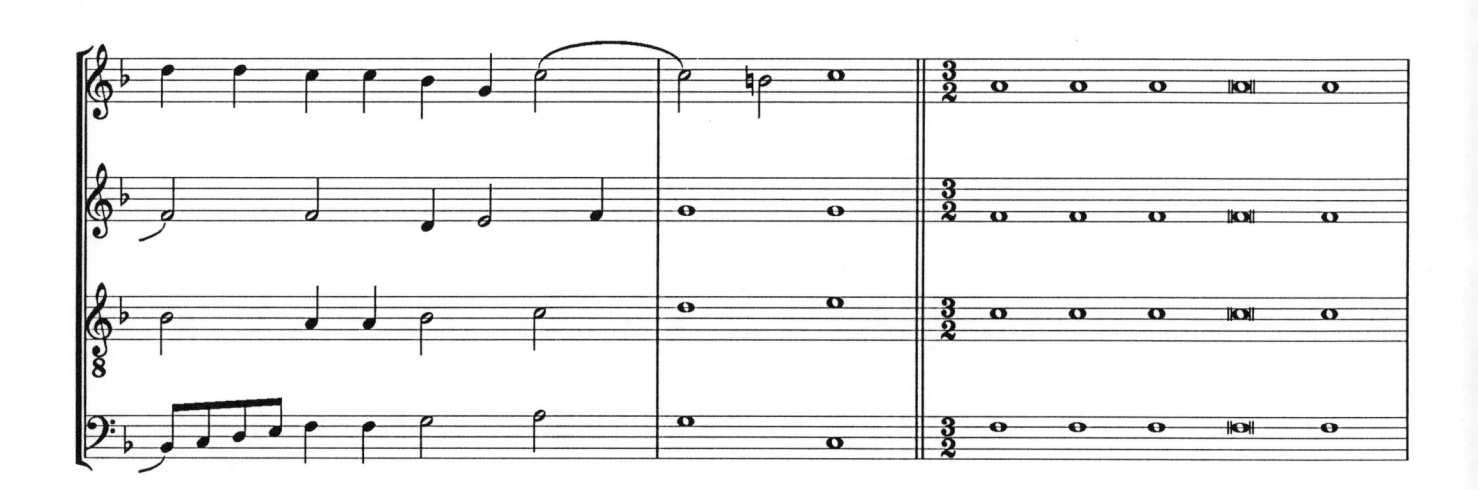

CANZON OTTAVA, LA GRASSA 55

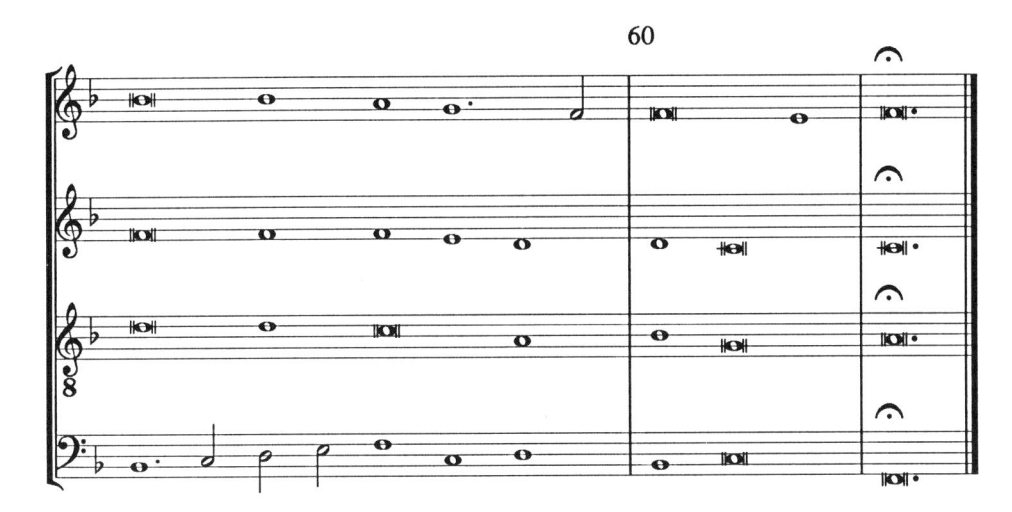

9. Canzon nona, La Theorica

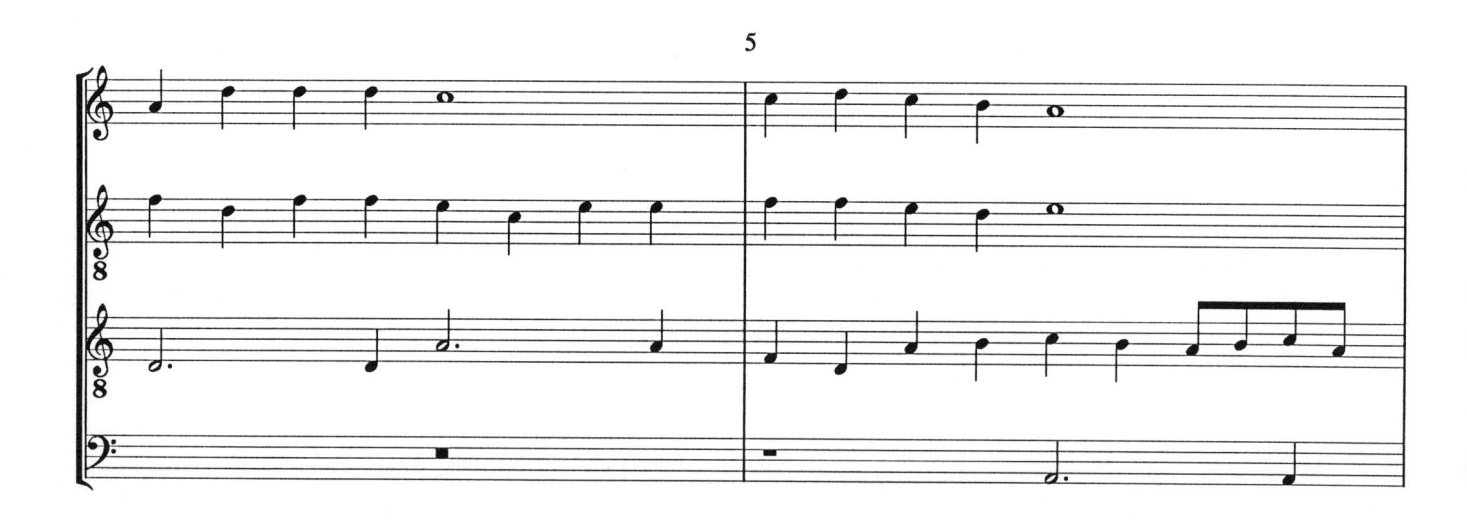

CANZON NONA, LA THEORICA 57

58 Canzon nona, La Theorica

CANZON NONA, LA THEORICA 59

60 CANZON NONA, LA THEORICA

CANZON NONA, LA THEORICA   61

Canzon nona, La Theorica

10. Canzon decima, La Guerra

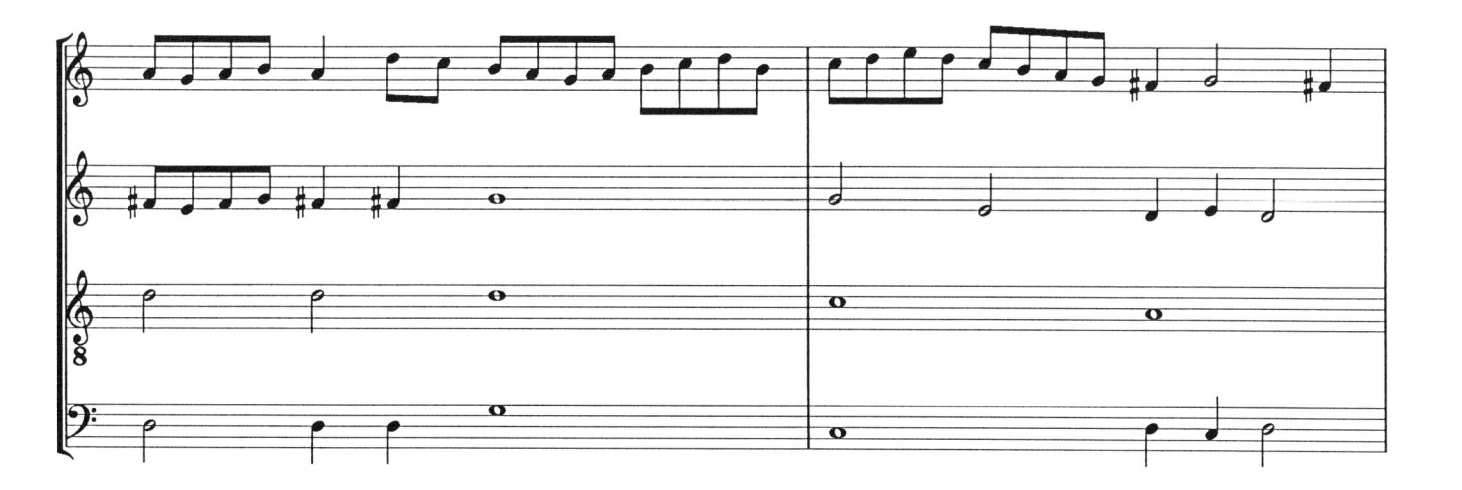

Canzon decima, La Guerra

CANZON DECIMA, LA GUERRA 65

66 Canzon decima, La Guerra

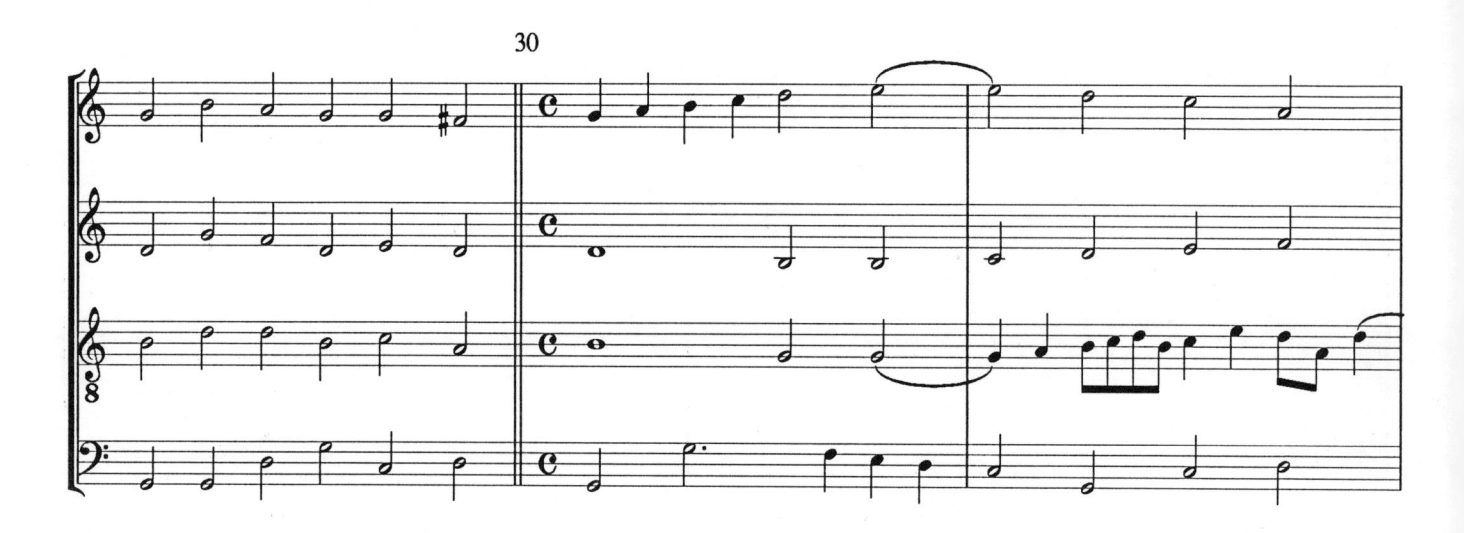

CANZON DECIMA, LA GUERRA 67

68 CANZON DECIMA, LA GUERRA

CANZON DECIMA, LA GUERRA 69

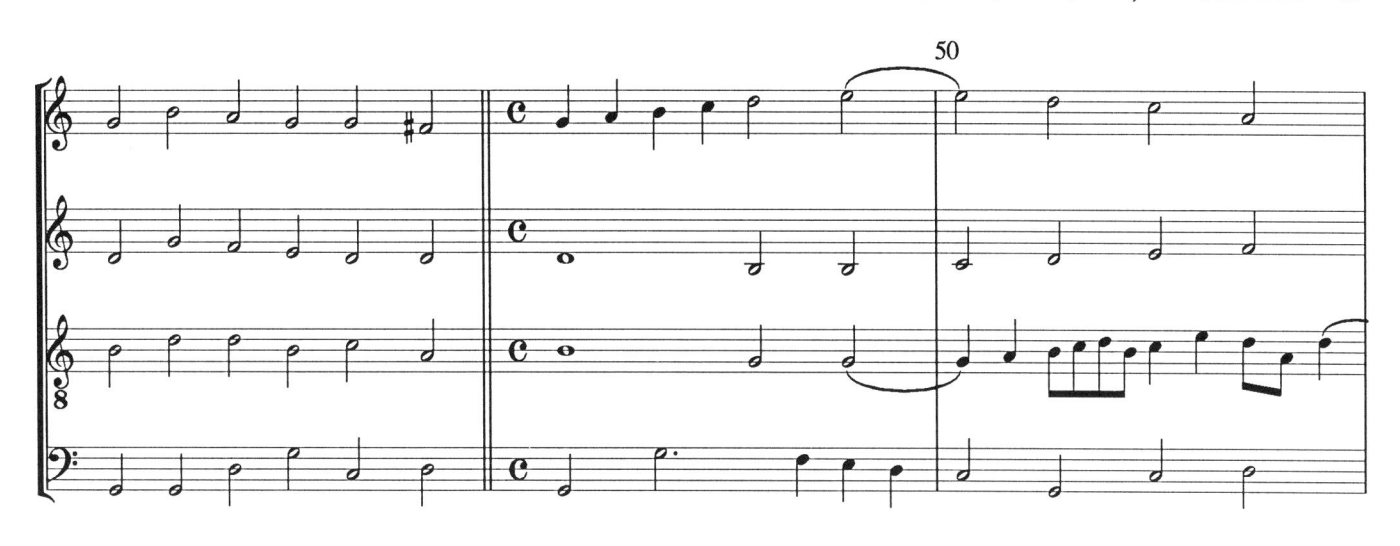

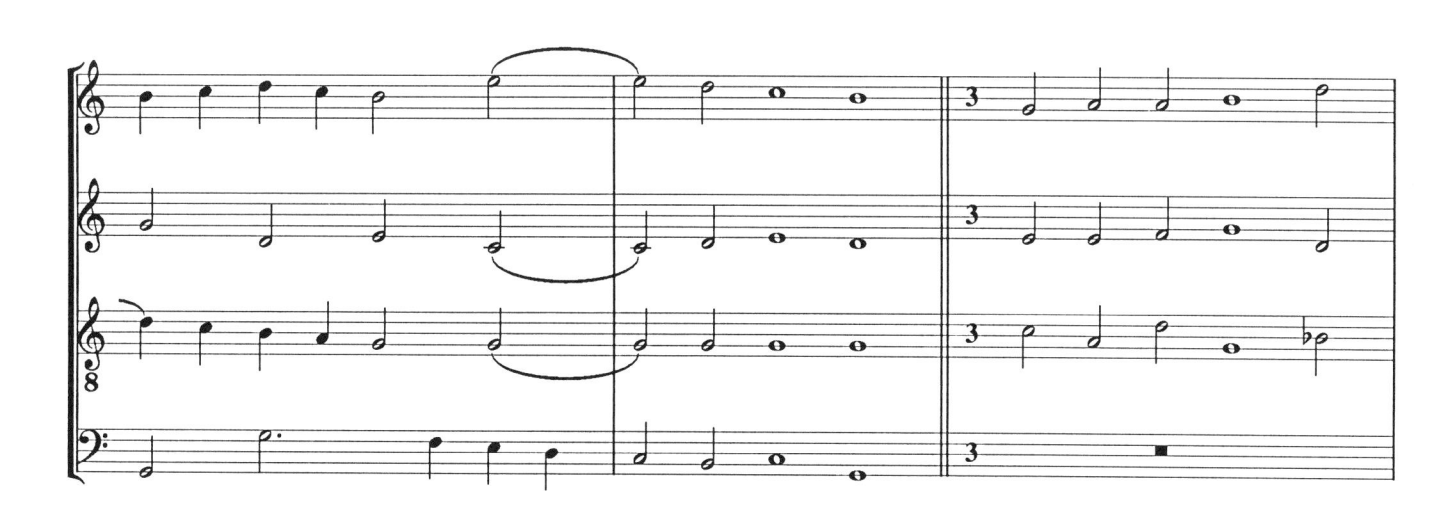

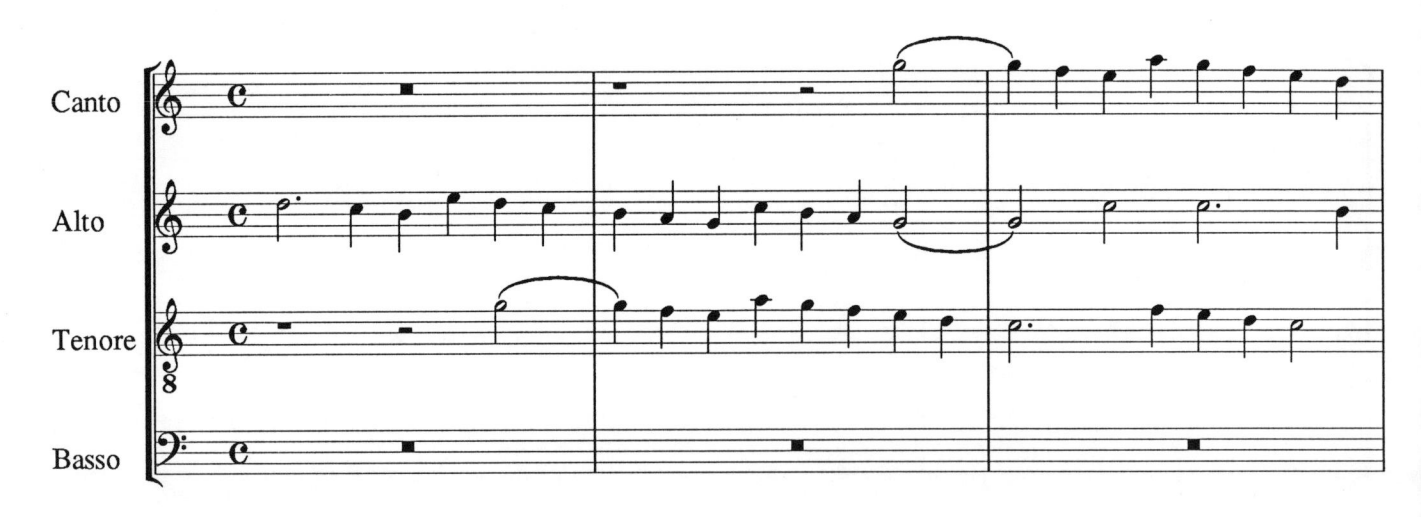

11. Canzon undecima, La Capitania

CANZON UNDECIMA, LA CAPITANIA 71

72 CANZON UNDECIMA, LA CAPITANIA

CANZON UNDECIMA, LA CAPITANIA 73

74 CANZON UNDECIMA, LA CAPITANIA

Canzon undecima, La Capitania

76 CANZON UNDECIMA, LA CAPITANIA

CANZON UNDECIMA, LA CAPITANIA

78 CANZON UNDECIMA, LA CAPITANIA

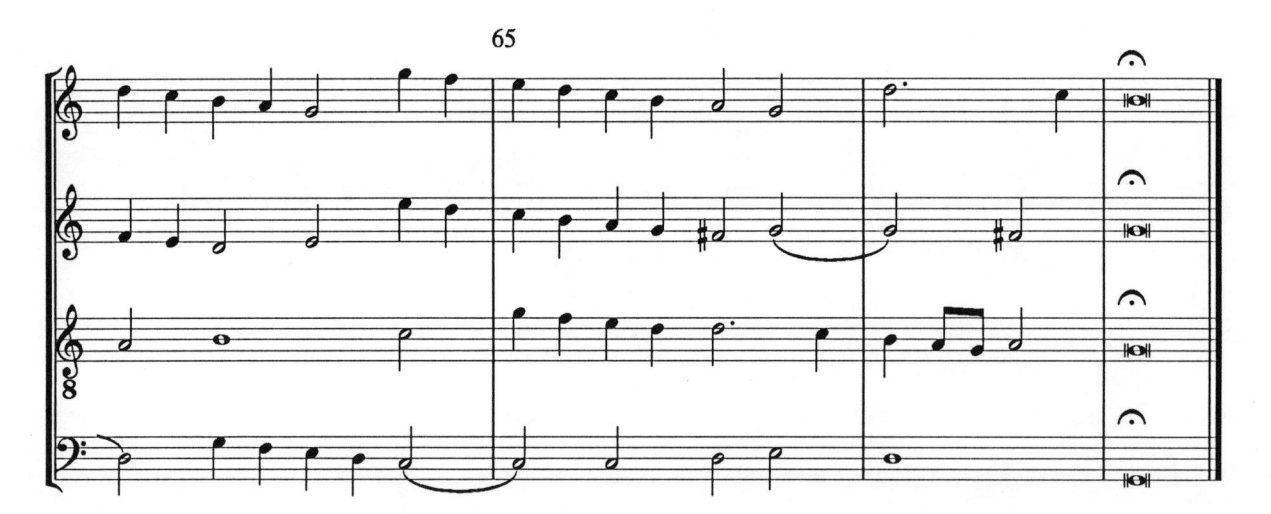

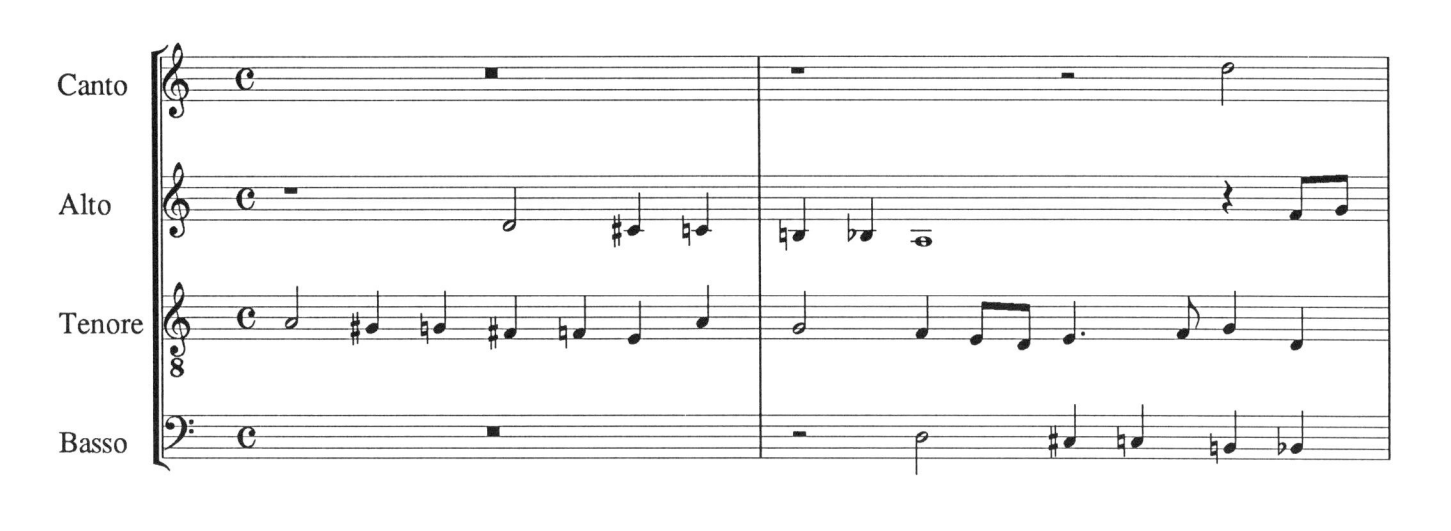

12. Canzon duodecima, La Bassa

80   Canzon duodecima, La Bassa

Canzon duodecima, La Bassa

82 Canzon duodecima, La Bassa

Canzon duodecima, La Bassa

84 CANZON DUODECIMA, LA BASSA

CANZON DUODECIMA, LA BASSA 85

86 CANZON DUODECIMA, LA BASSA

CANZON DUODECIMA, LA BASSA 87

88 Canzon duodecima, La Bassa

13. Canzon decimaterza, La Torta

90 Canzon decimaterza, La Torta

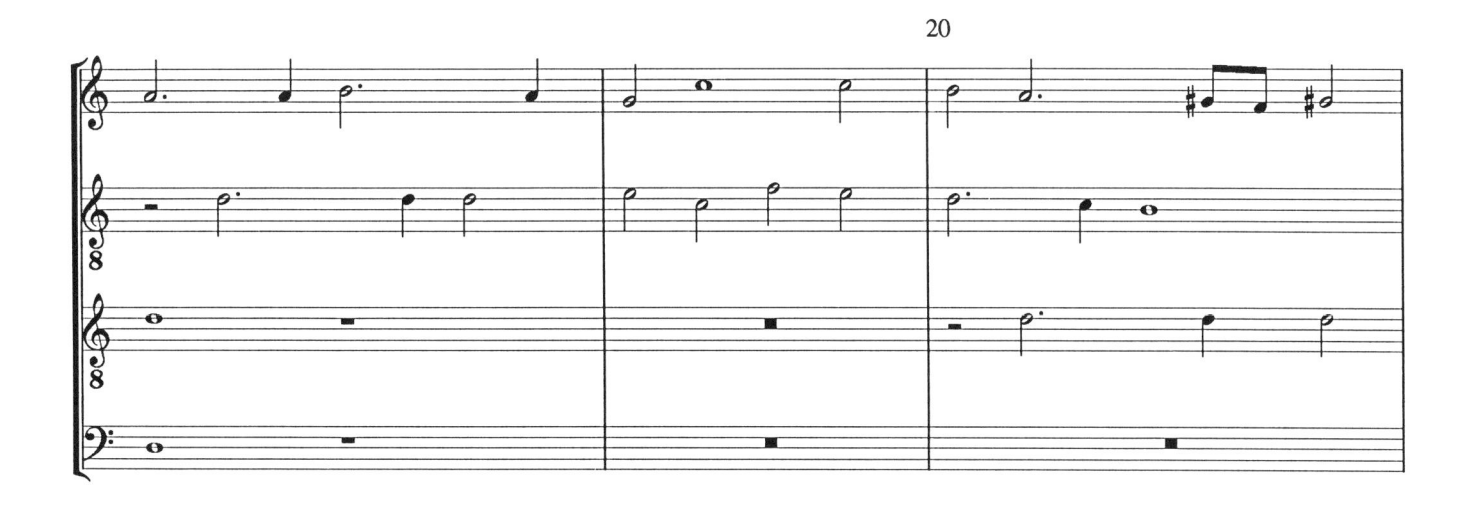

CANZON DECIMATERZA, LA TORTA 91

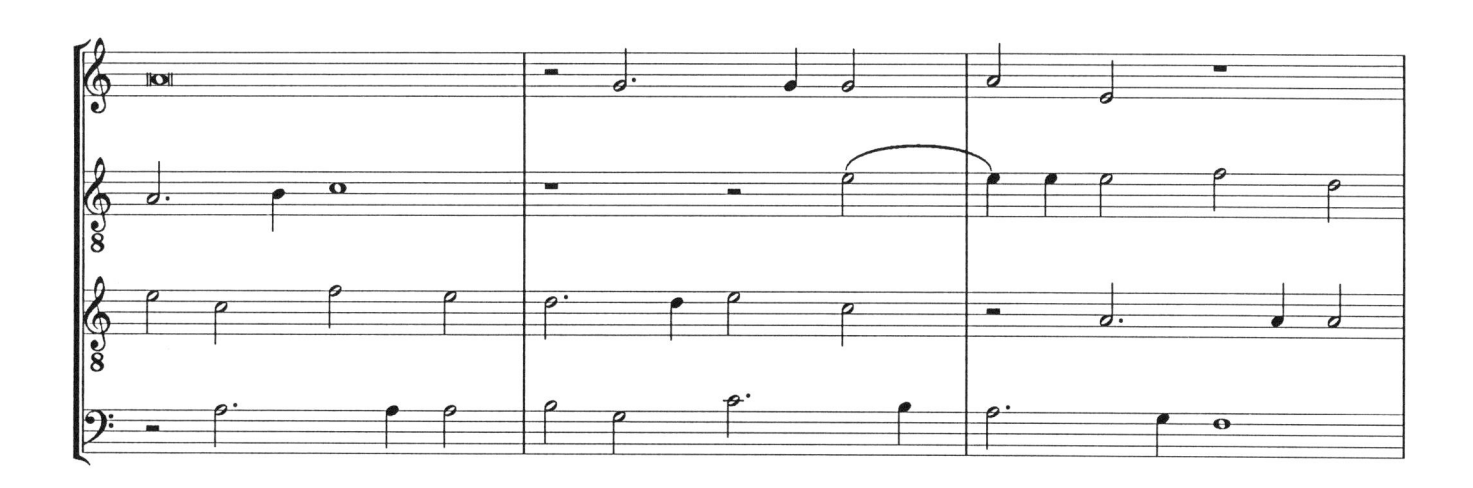

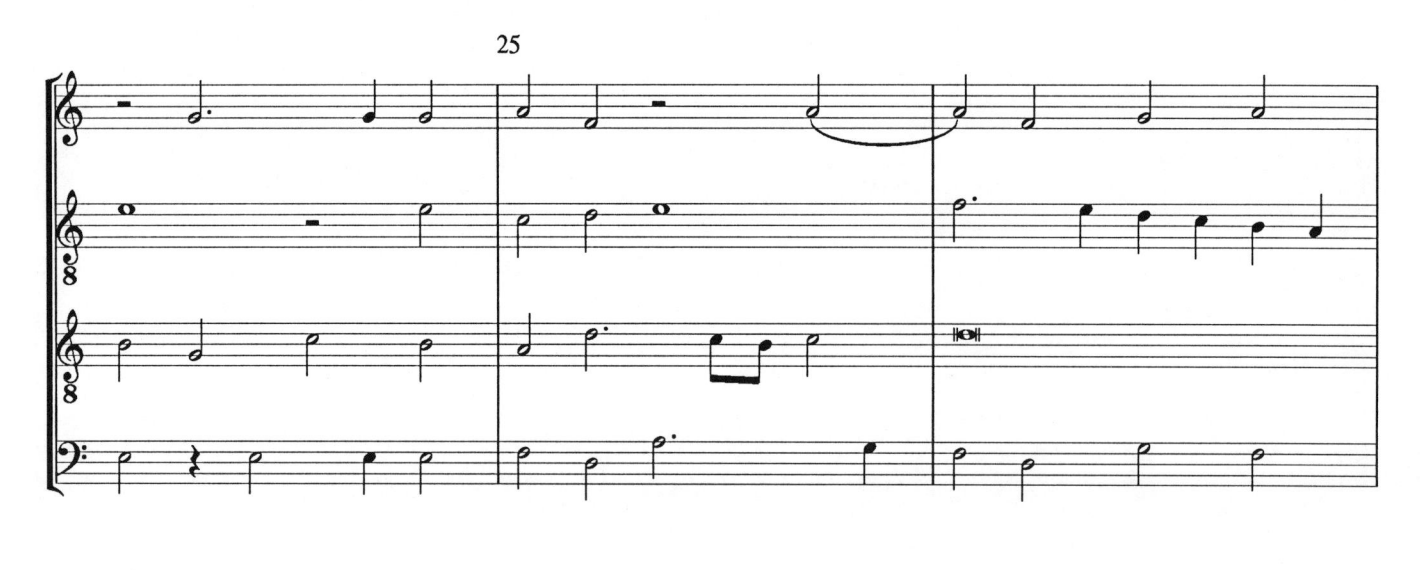

92 CANZON DECIMATERZA, LA TORTA

CANZON DECIMATERZA, LA TORTA

94 CANZON DECIMATERZA, LA TORTA

CANZON DECIMATERZA, LA TORTA 95

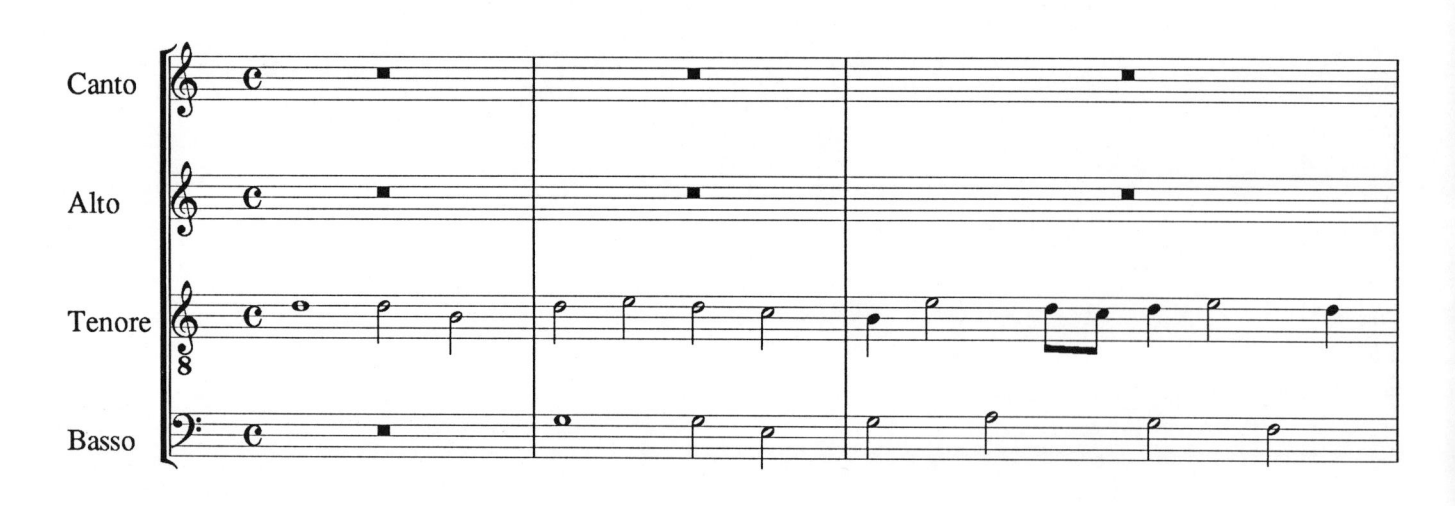

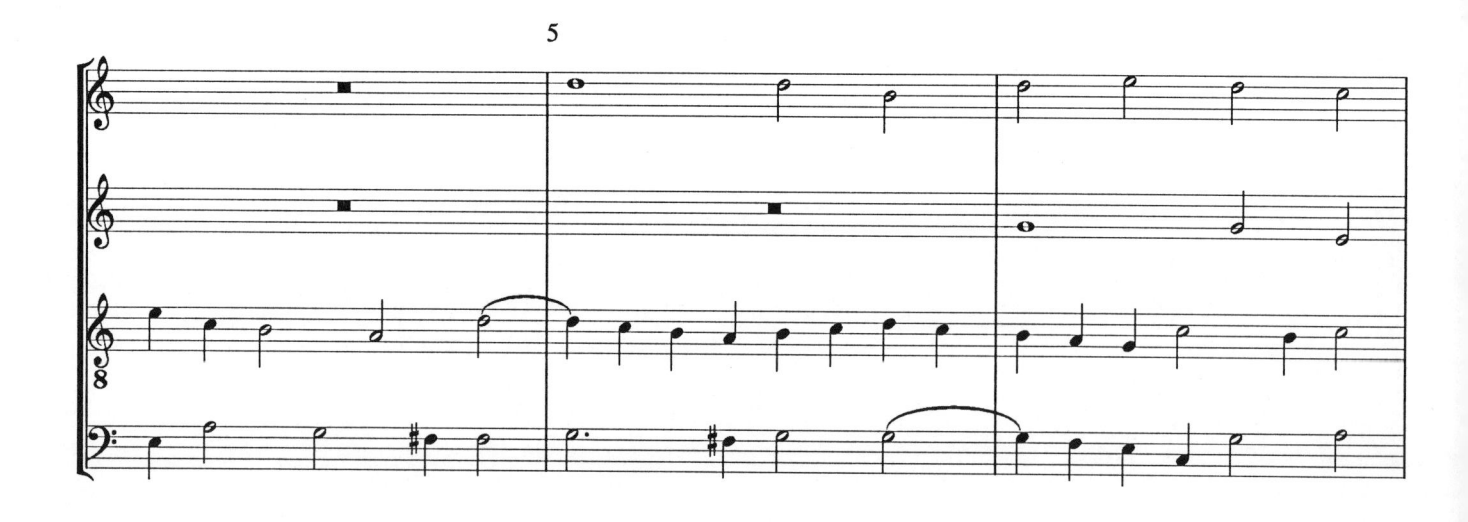

14. Canzon decimaquarta, La Filippa

CANZON DECIMAQUARTA, LA FILIPPA 97

98 Canzon decimaquarta, La Filippa

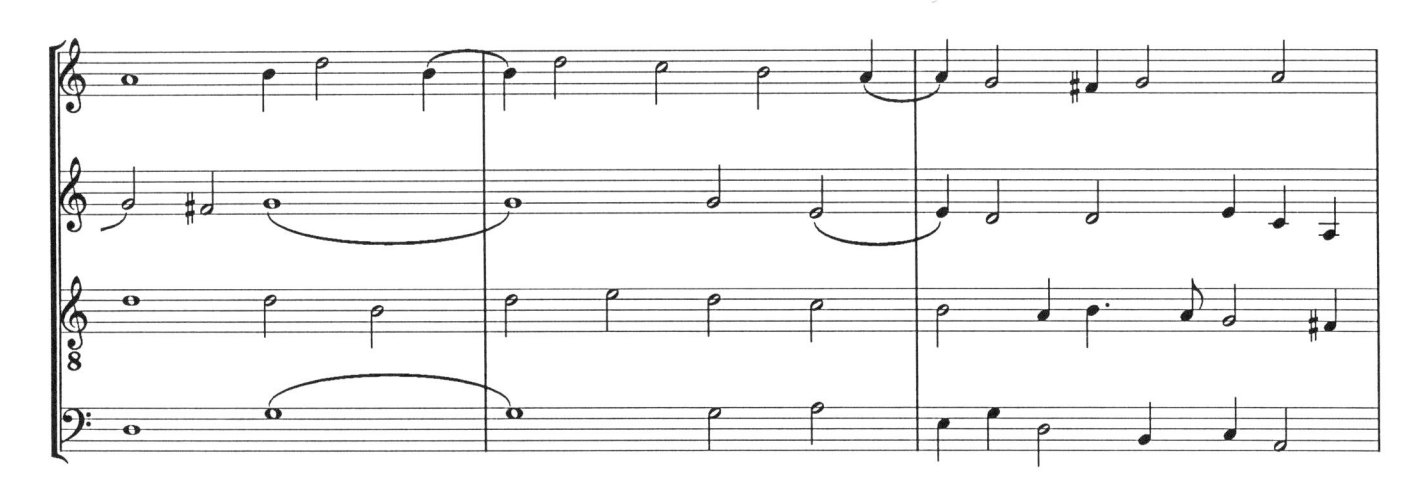

CANZON DECIMAQUARTA, LA FILIPPA 99

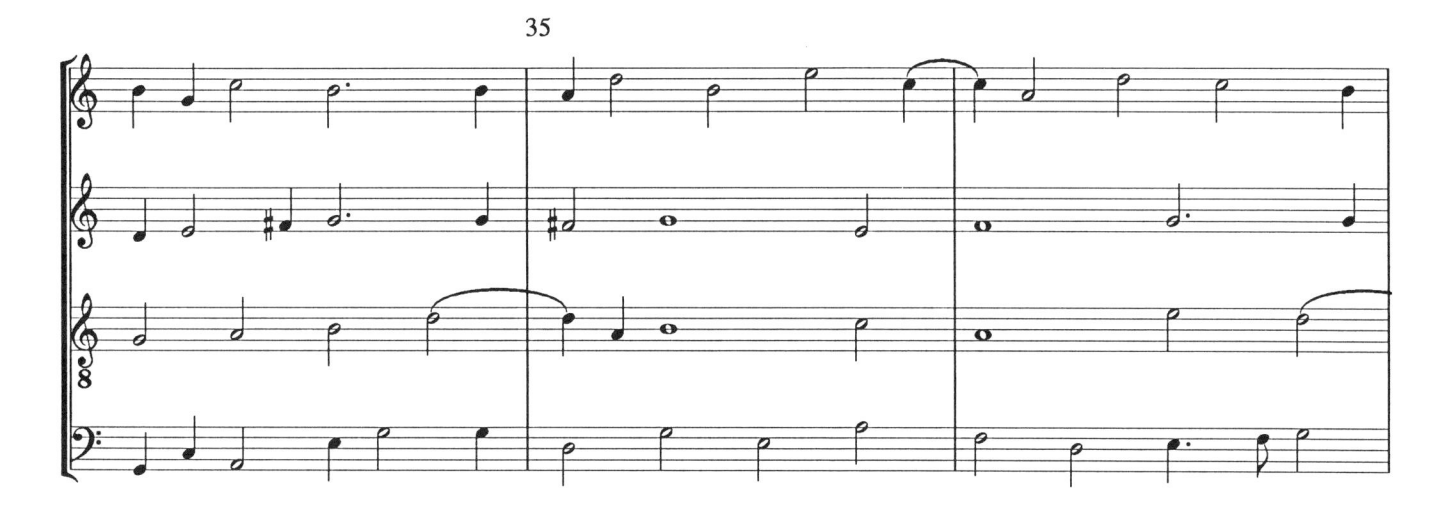

100 CANZON DECIMAQUARTA, LA FILIPPA

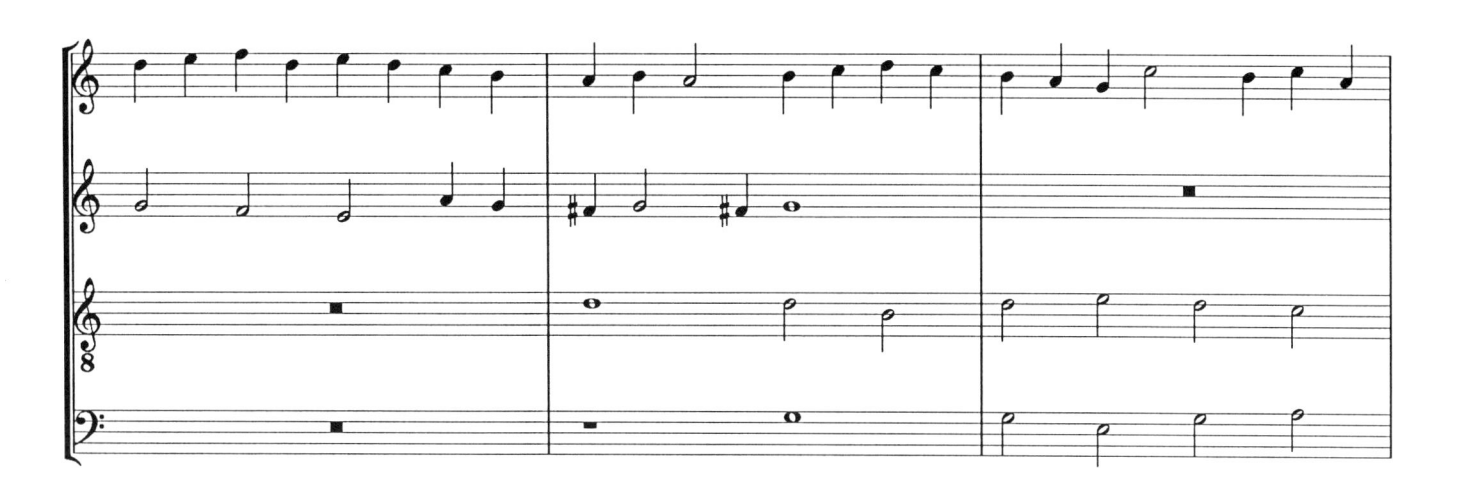

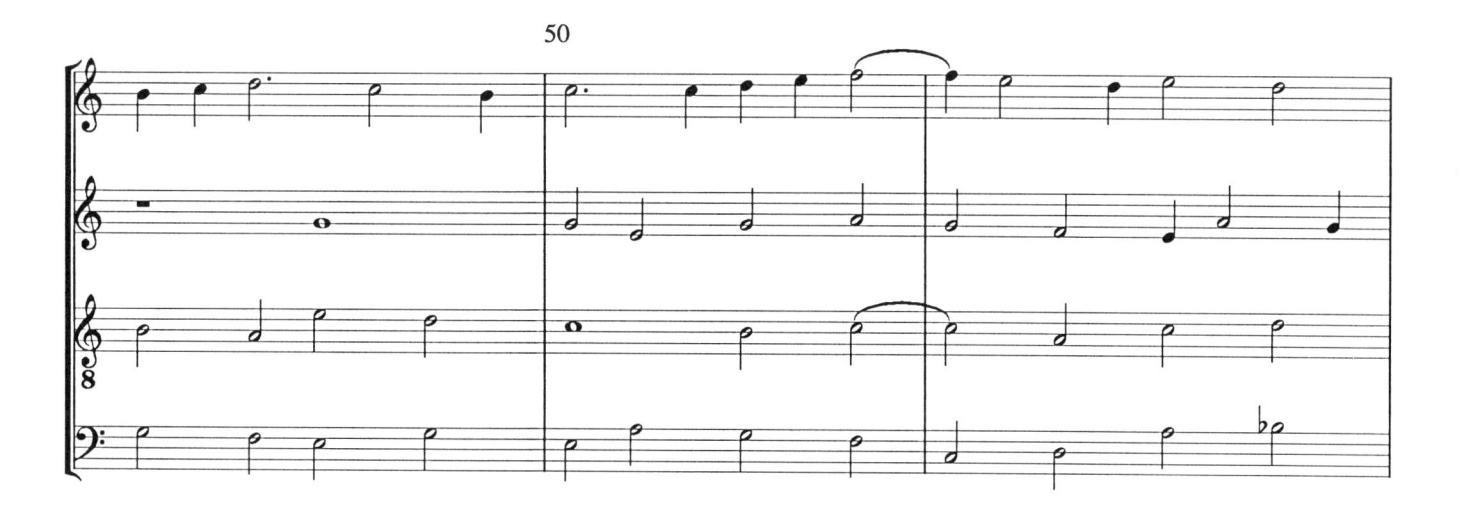

CANZON DECIMAQUARTA, LA FILIPPA 101

102 CANZON DECIMAQUARTA, LA FILIPPA

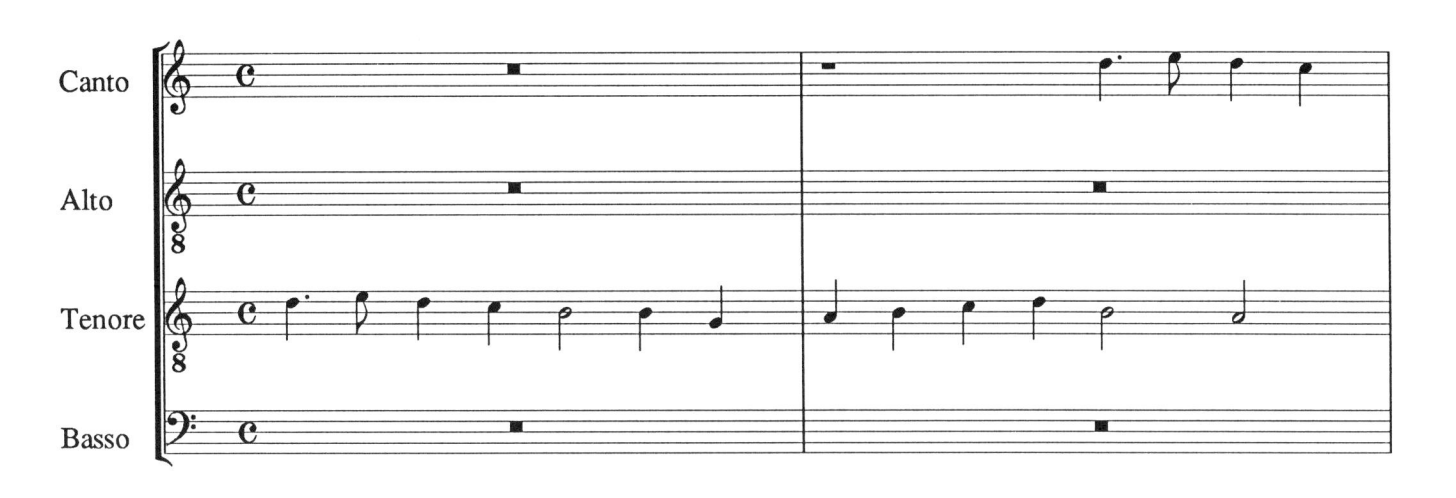

15. Canzon decimaquinta, La Fiorina

104   Canzon decimaquinta, La Fiorina

CANZON DECIMAQUINTA, LA FIORINA 105

Canzon decimaquinta, La Fiorina

CANZON DECIMAQUINTA, LA FIORINA 107

108 CANZON DECIMAQUINTA, LA FIORINA

CANZON DECIMAQUINTA, LA FIORINA 109

110 Canzon decimaquinta, La Fiorina

CANZON DECIMAQUINTA, LA FIORINA 111

16. Canzon decimasesta, La Girometta

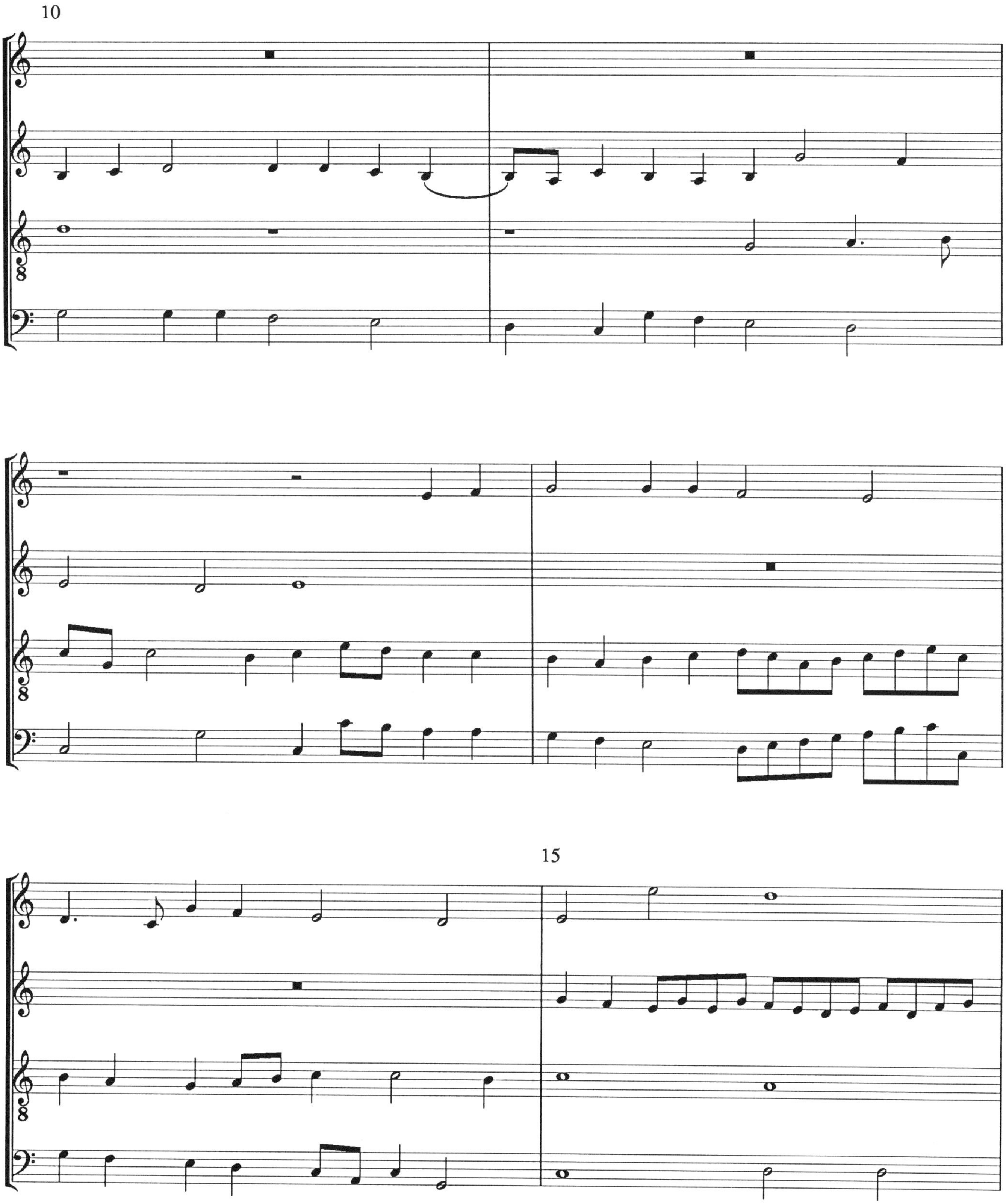
10
15

114 Canzon decimasesta, La Girometta

CANZON DECIMASESTA, LA GIROMETTA

116 CANZON DECIMASESTA, LA GIROMETTA

CANZON DECIMASESTA, LA GIROMETTA 117

118 CANZON DECIMASESTA, LA GIROMETTA

CANZON DECIMASESTA, LA GIROMETTA 119

17. Canzon decimasettima, La Genovesa

CANZON DECIMASETTIMA, LA GENOVESA   121

122 Canzon decimasettima, La Genovesa

CANZON DECIMASETTIMA, LA GENOVESA

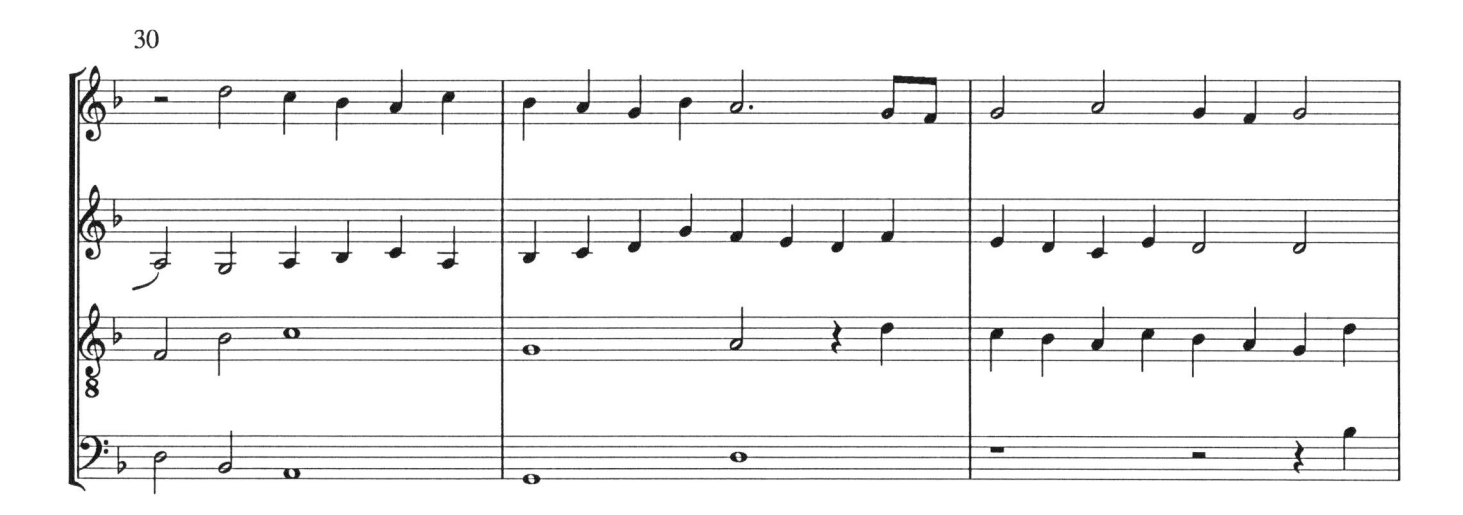

124 Canzon decimasettima, La Genovesa

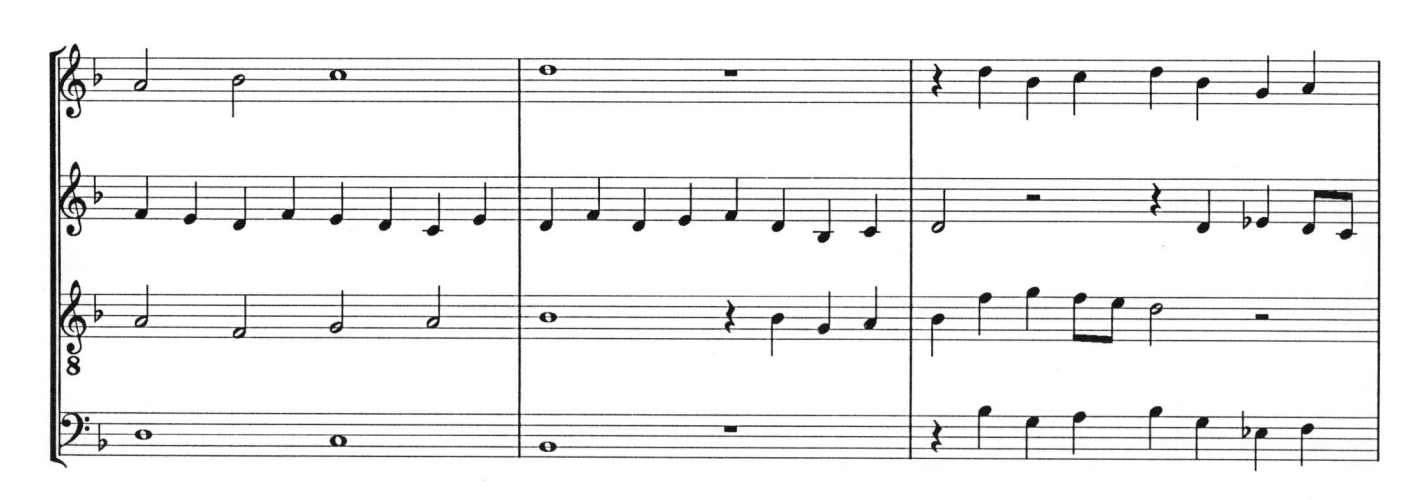

CANZON DECIMASETTIMA, LA GENOVESA

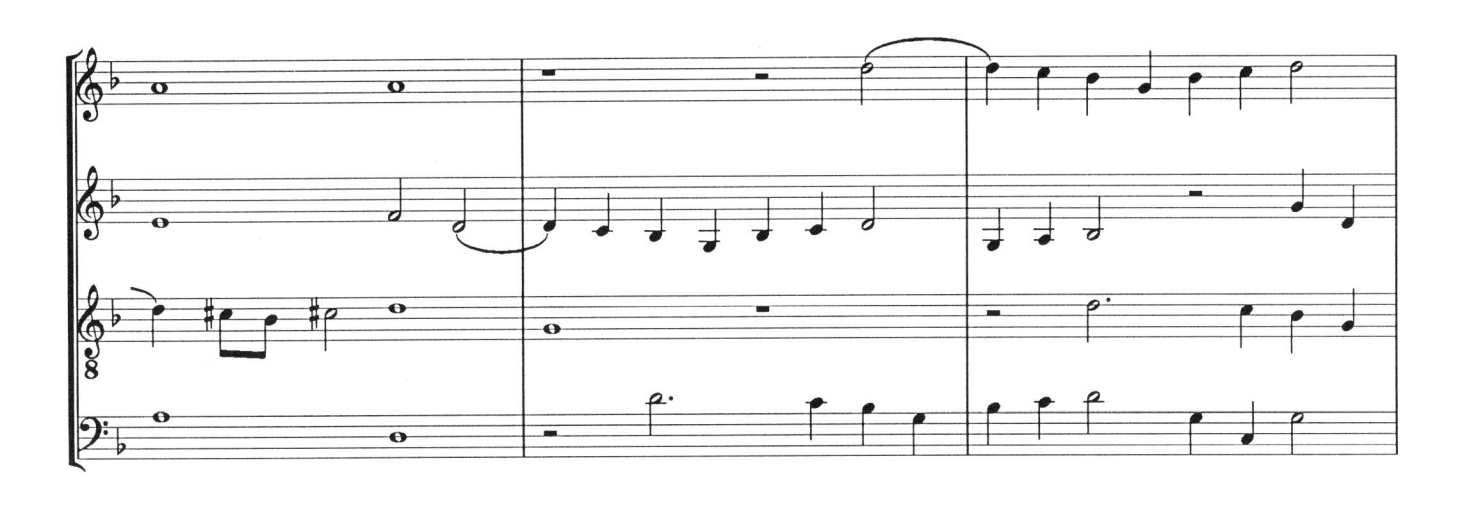

126 Canzon decimasettima, La Genovesa

CANZON DECIMASETTIMA, LA GENOVESA   127

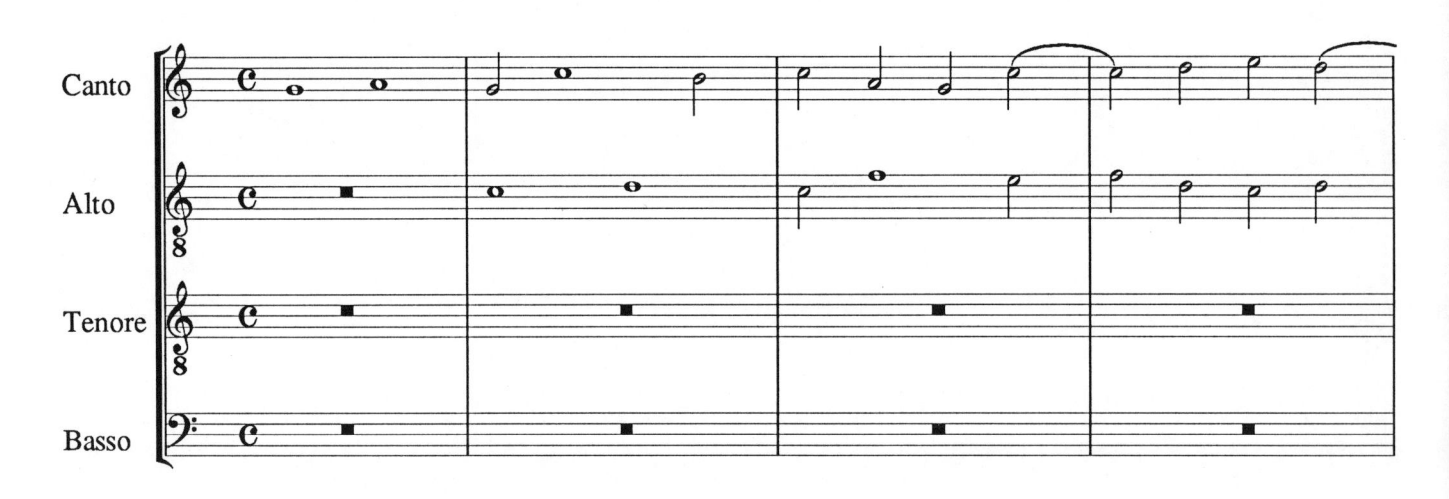

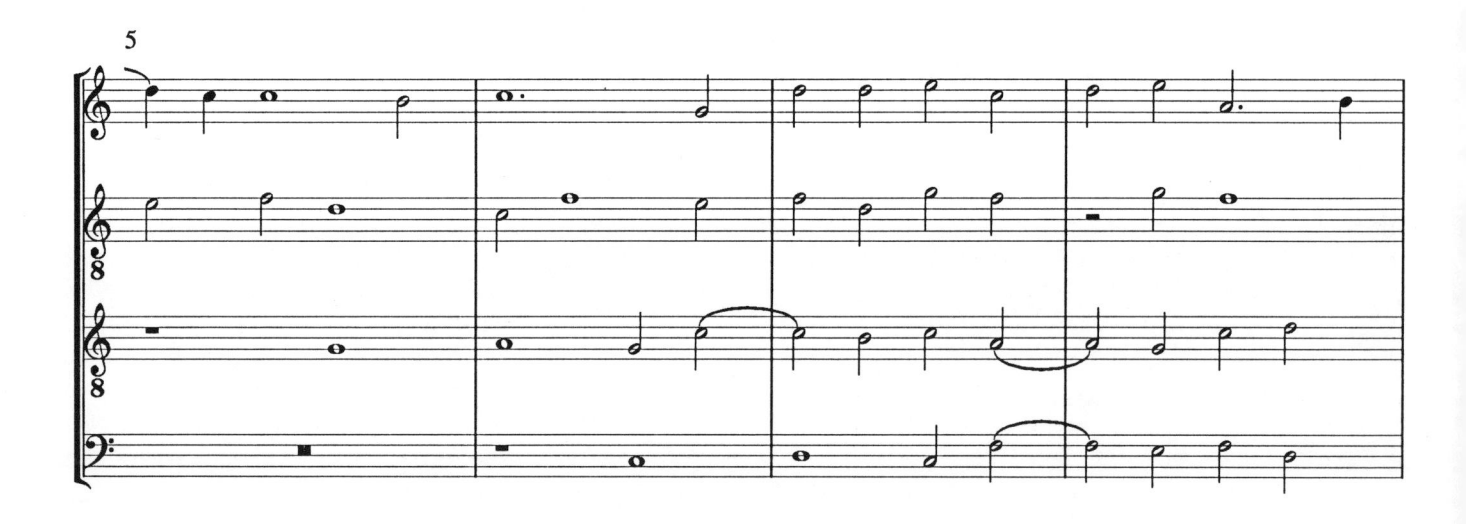

18. Canzon decimaottava, La Alessandrina

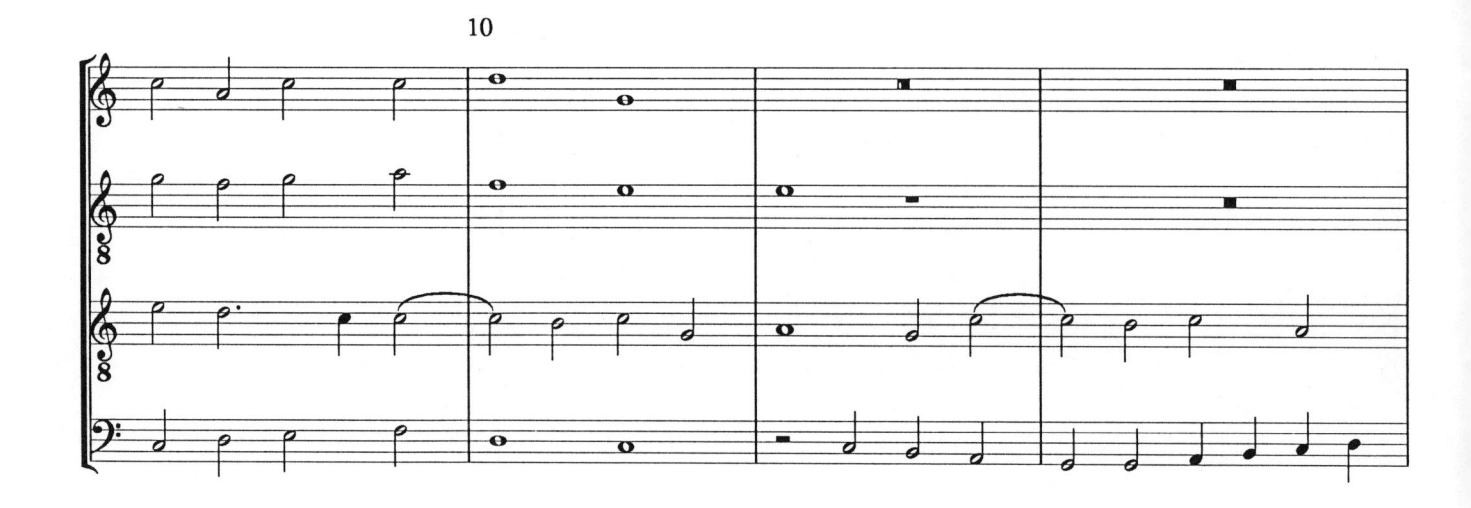

Canzon decimaottava, La Alessandrina

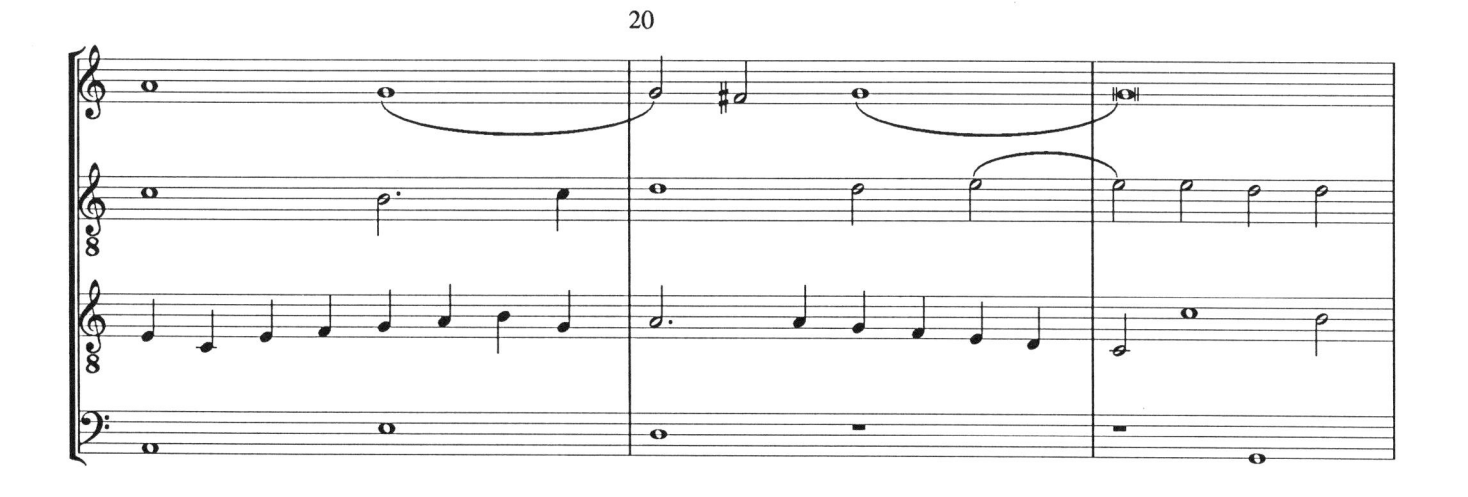

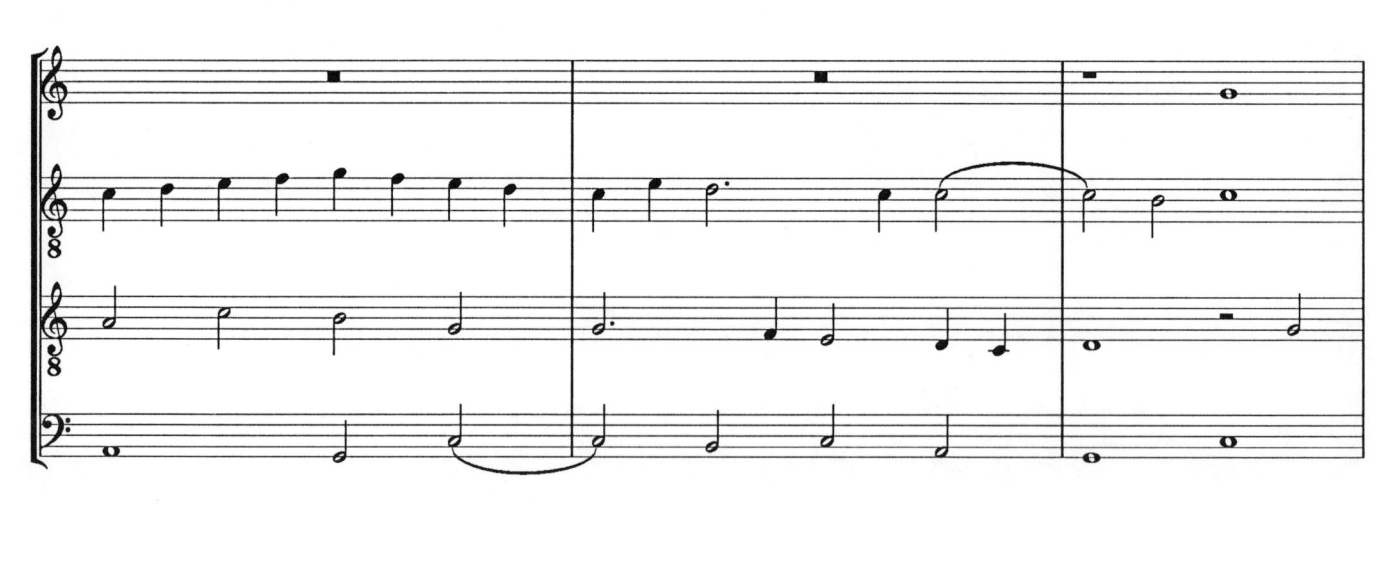

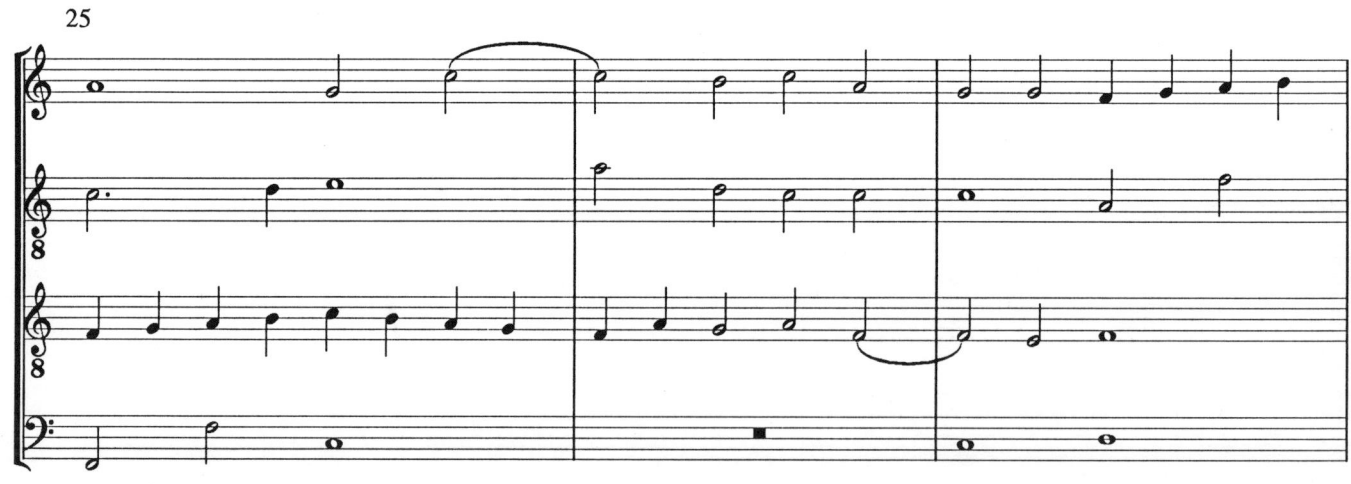

130 Canzon decimaottava, La Alessandrina

Canzon decimaottava, La Alessandrina

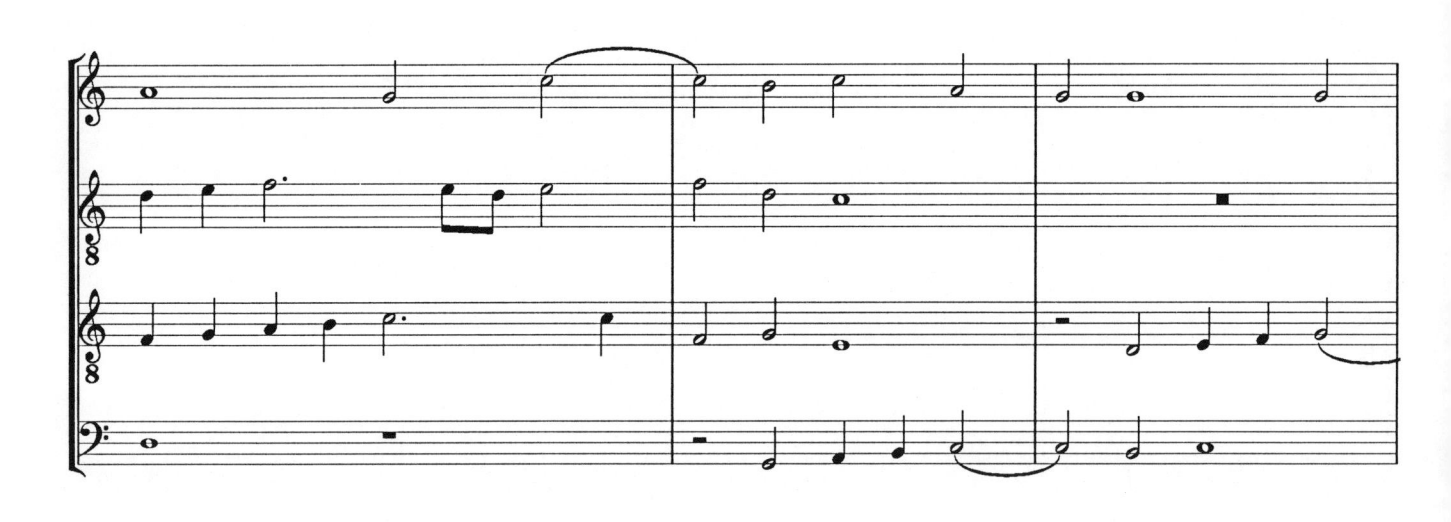

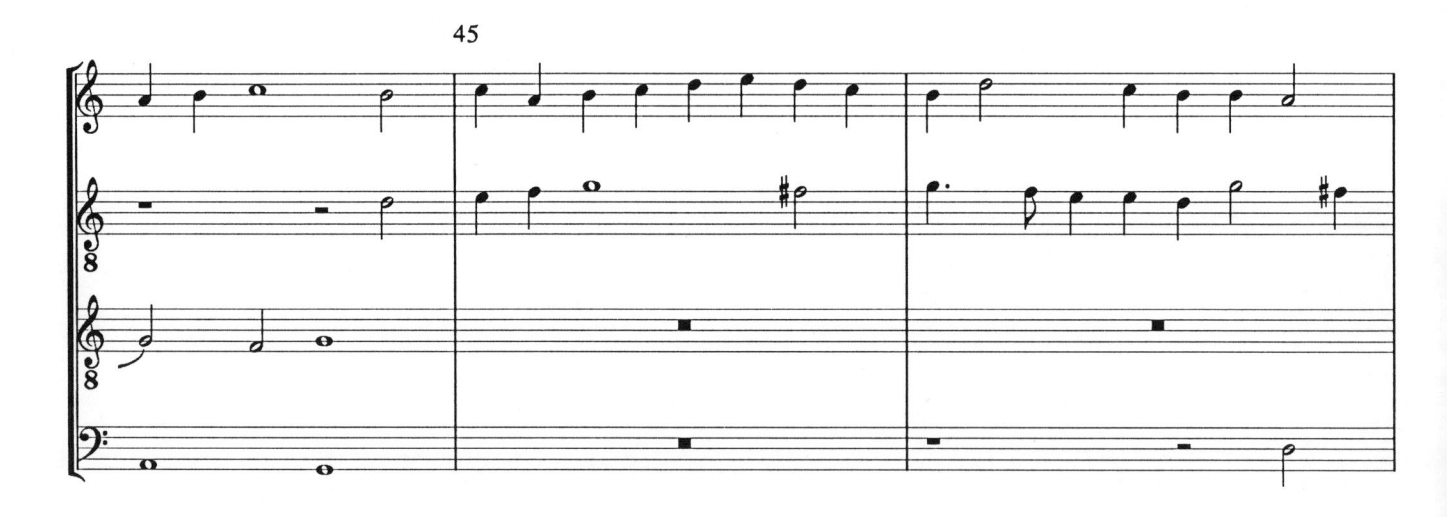

132 Canzon decimaottava, La Alessandrina

CANZON DECIMAOTTAVA, LA ALESSANDRINA

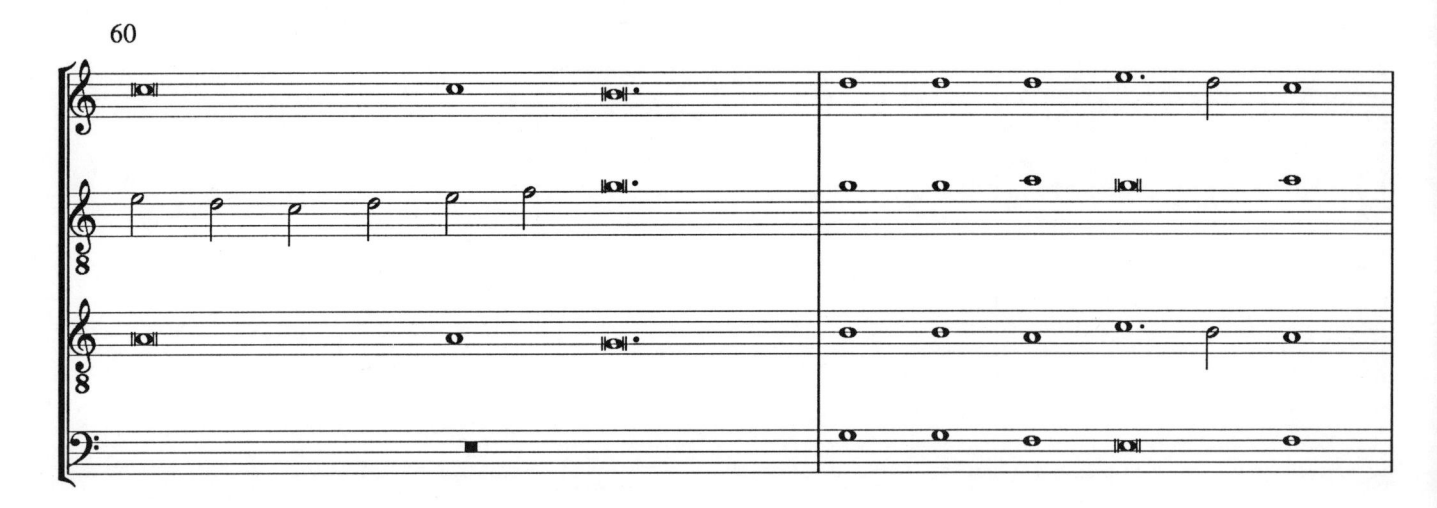

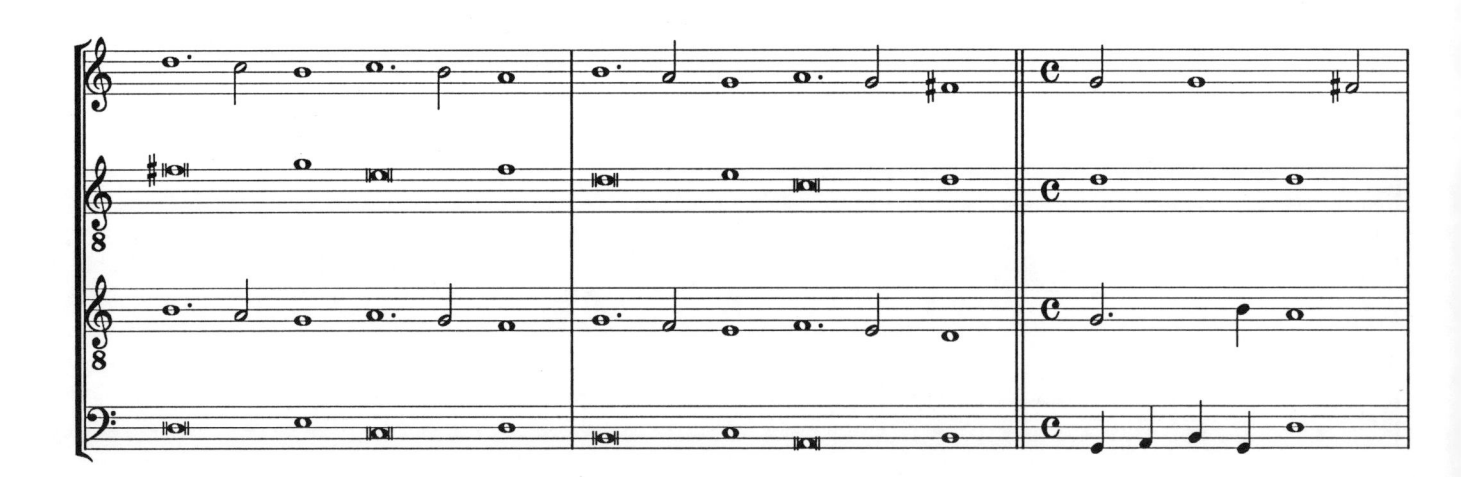

134 Canzon decimaottava, La Alessandrina

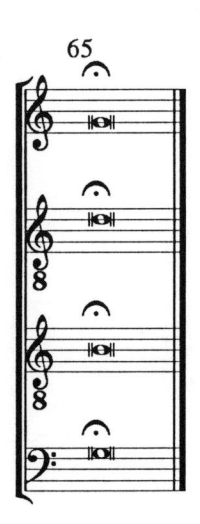

19. Canzon decimanona, La Confrata

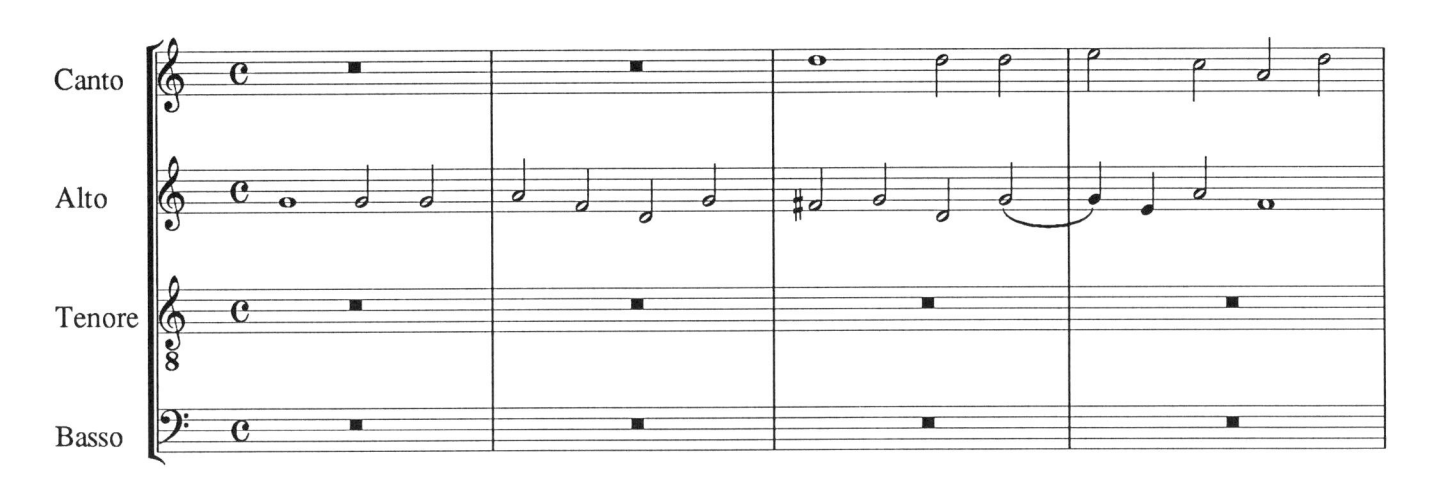

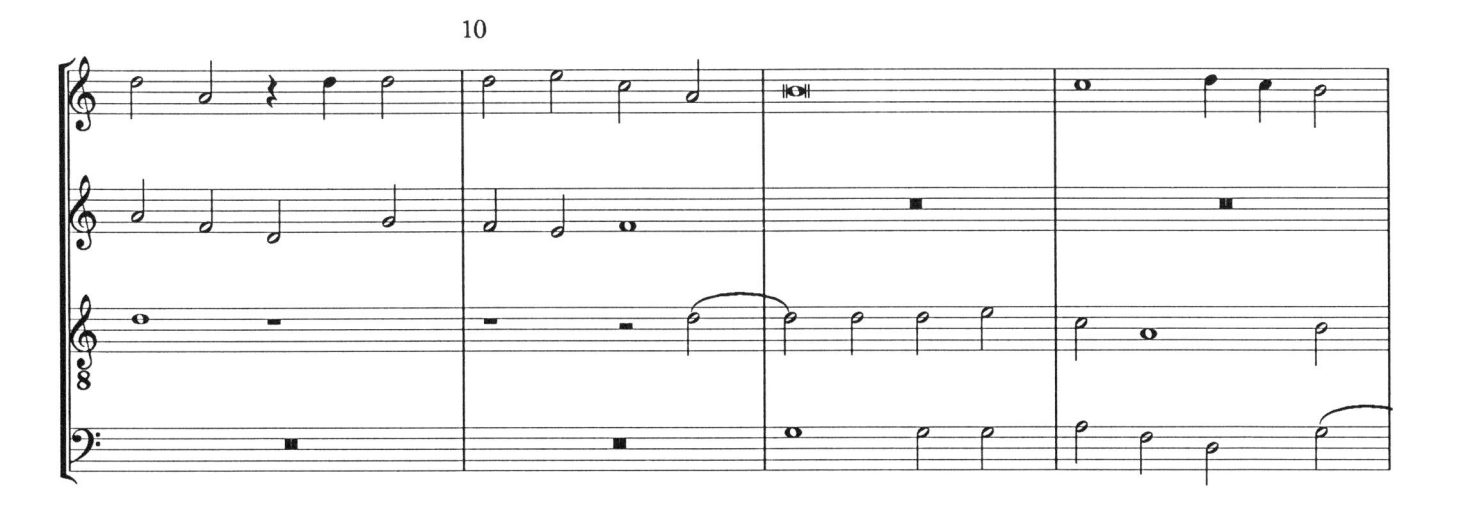

136 Canzon decimanona, La Confrata

CANZON DECIMANONA, LA CONFRATA

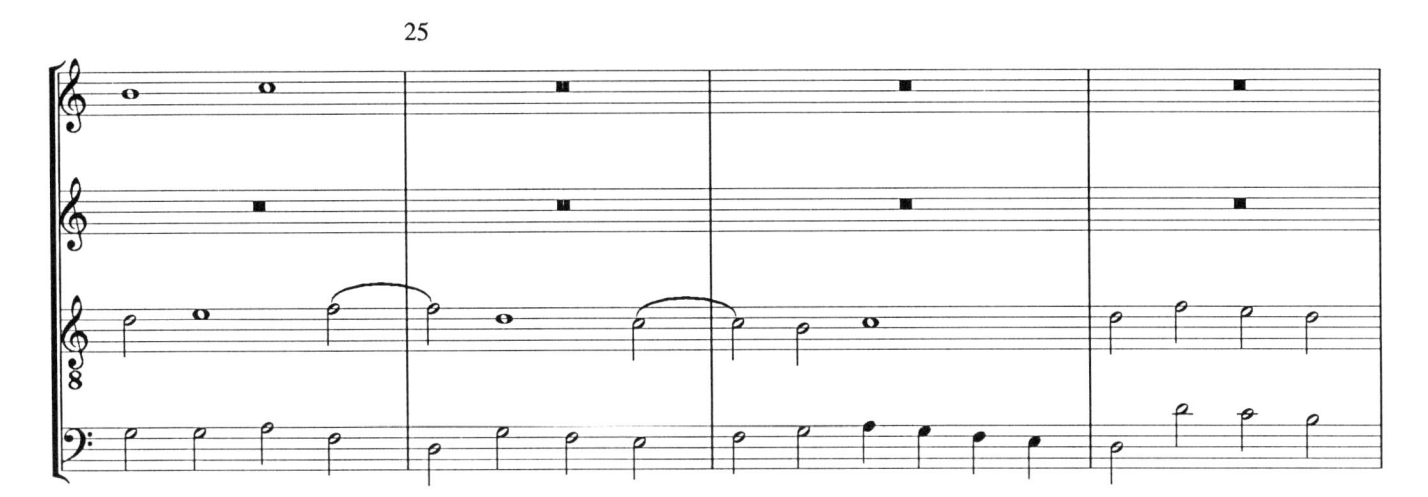

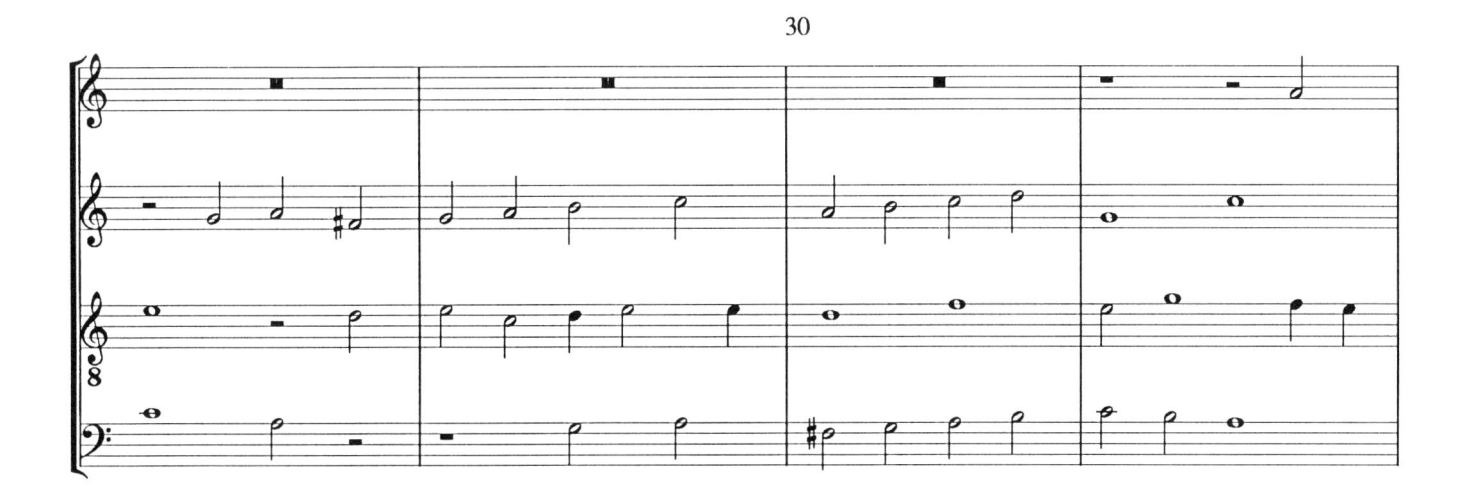

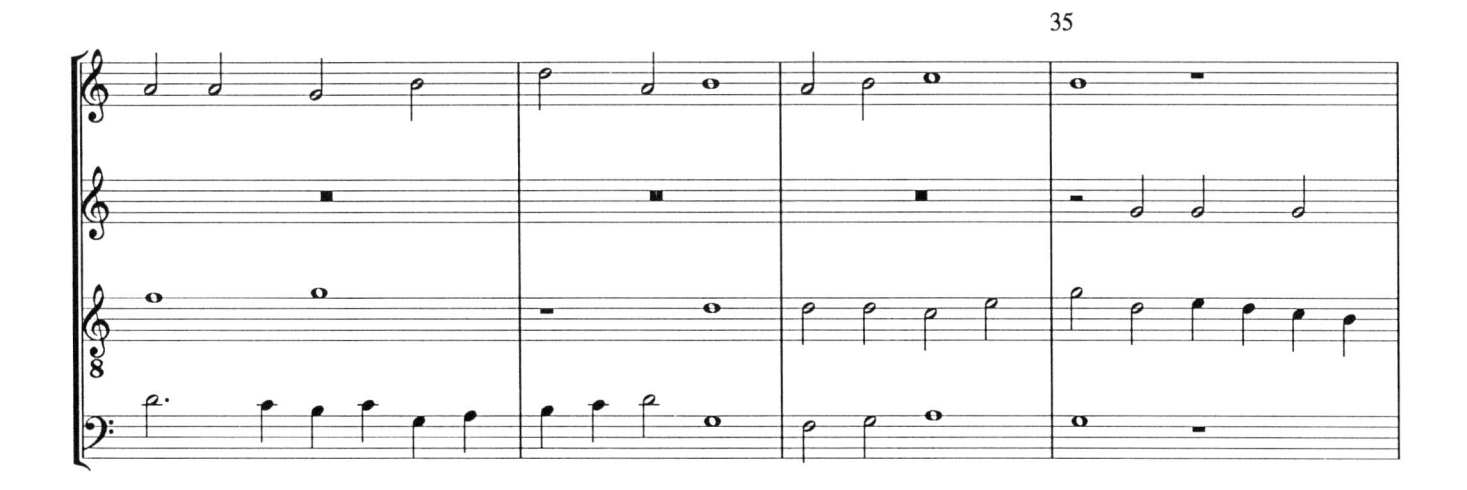

138 Canzon decimanona, La Confrata

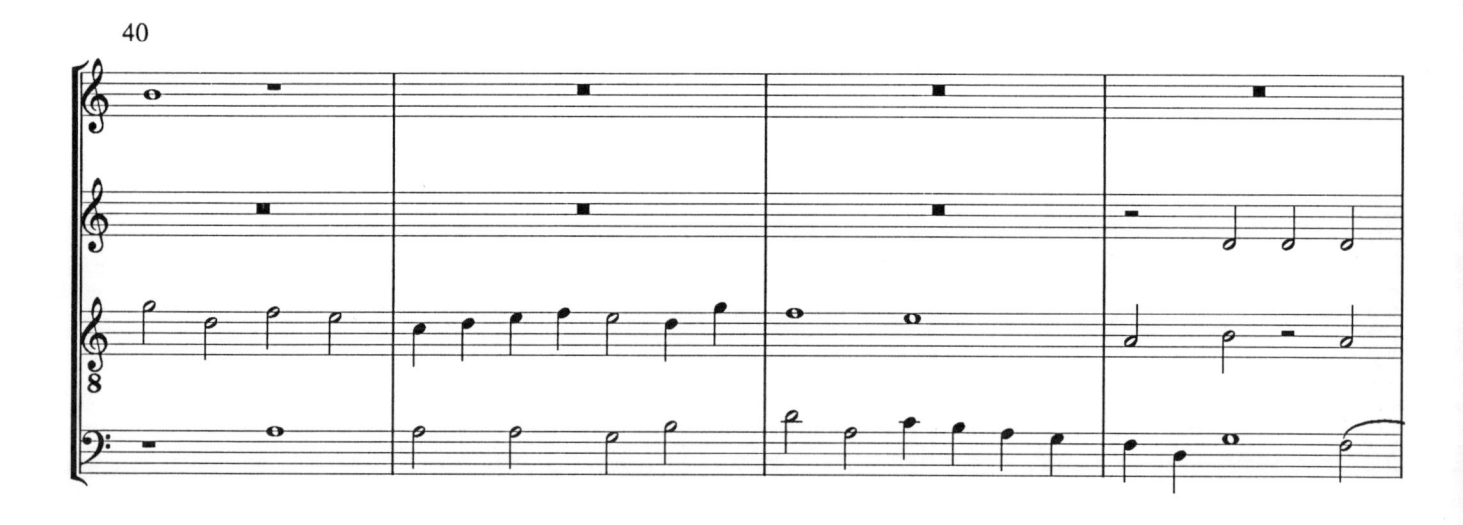

CANZON DECIMANONA, LA CONFRATA 139

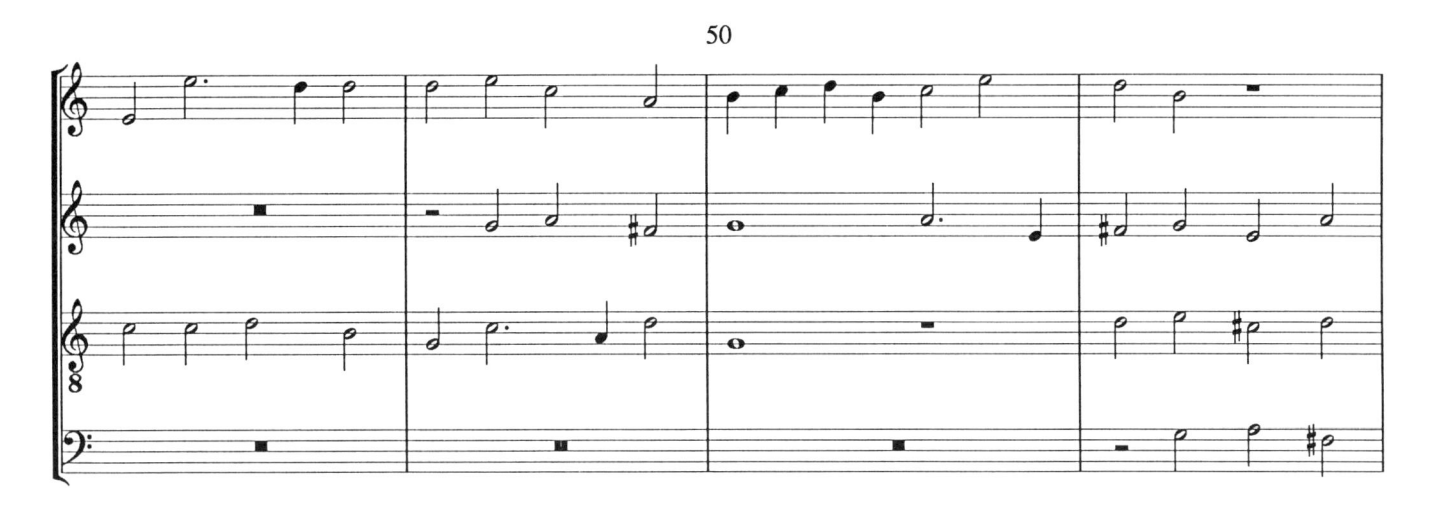

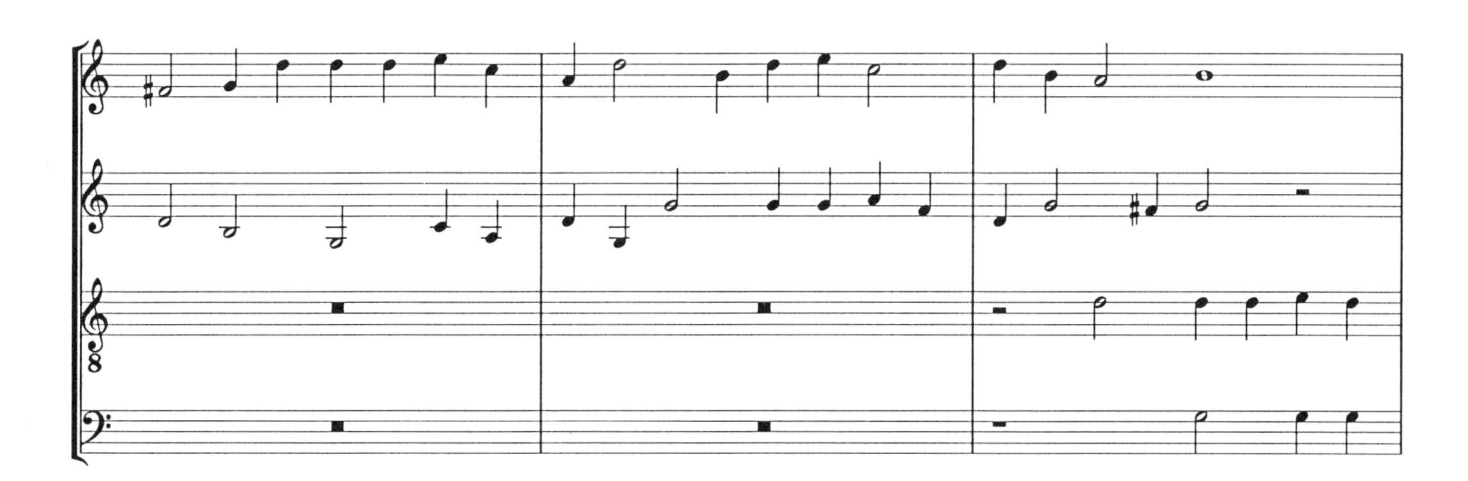

140 CANZON DECIMANONA, LA CONFRATA

CANZON DECIMANONA, LA CONFRATA 141

20. Canzon vigesima, La Furugada

CANZON VIGESIMA, LA FURUGADA 143

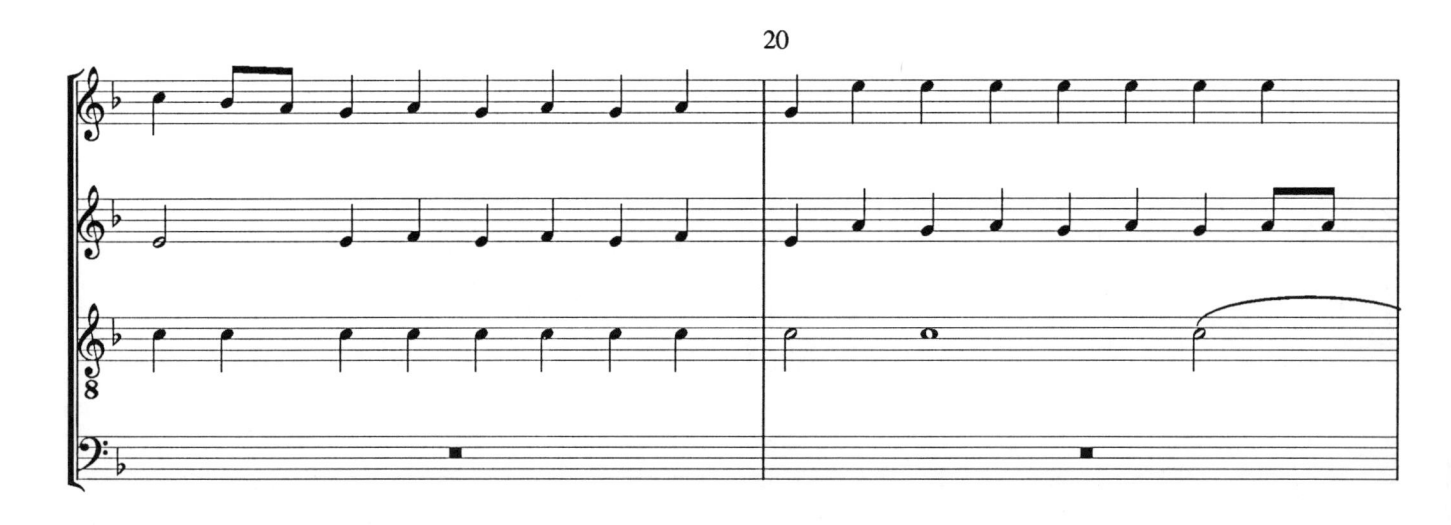

144 CANZON VIGESIMA, LA FURUGADA

CANZON VIGESIMA, LA FURUGADA   145

146 CANZON VIGESIMA, LA FURUGADA

CANZON VIGESIMA, LA FURUGADA 147

148 CANZON VIGESIMA, LA FURUGADA

CANZON VIGESIMA, LA FURUGADA 149

150 Canzon vigesima, La Furugada

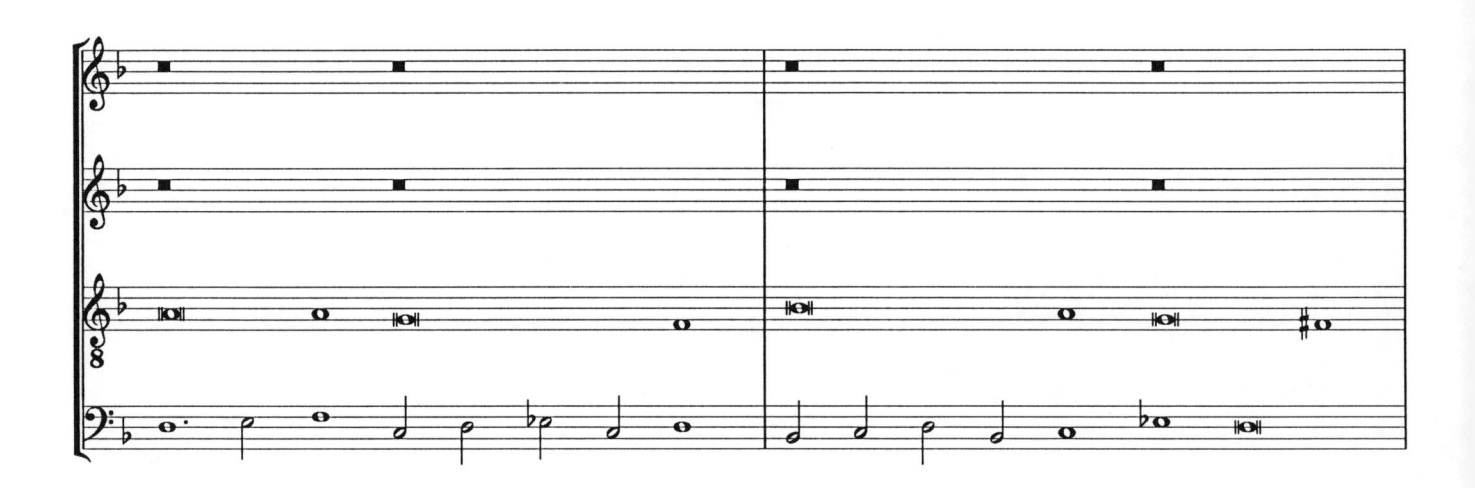

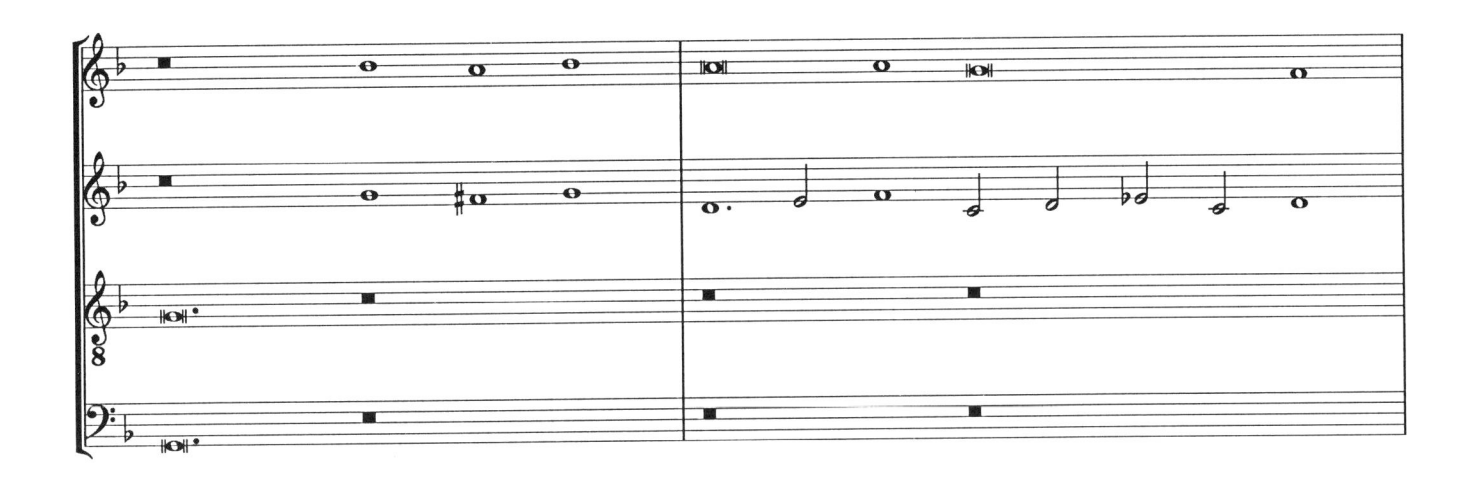

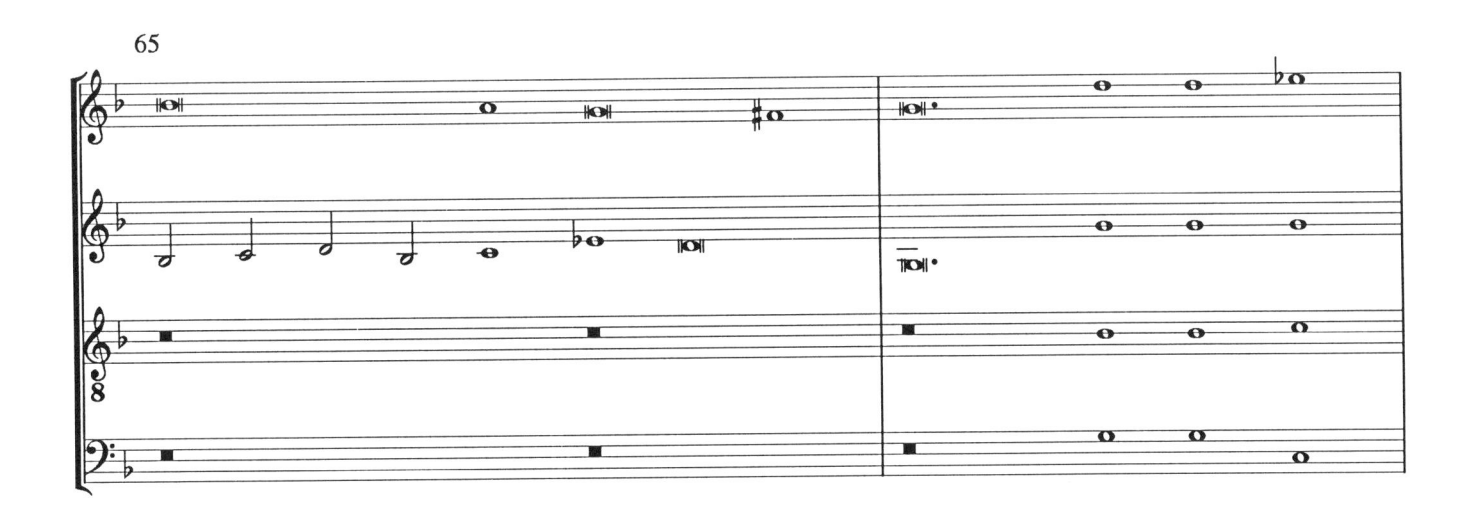

CANZON VIGESIMA, LA FURUGADA 151

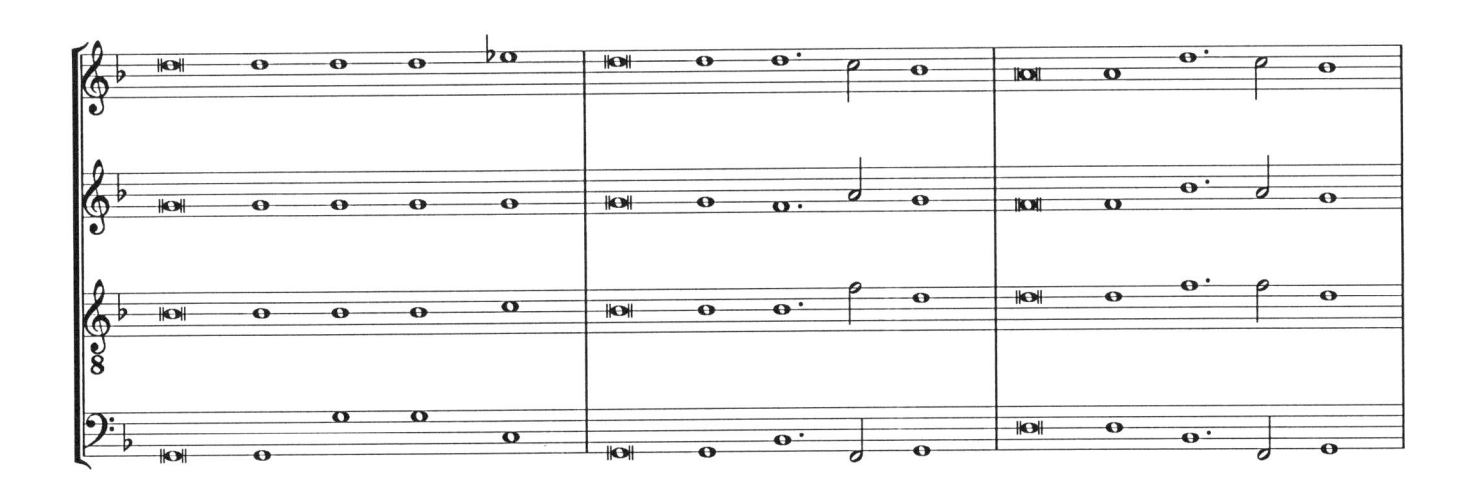

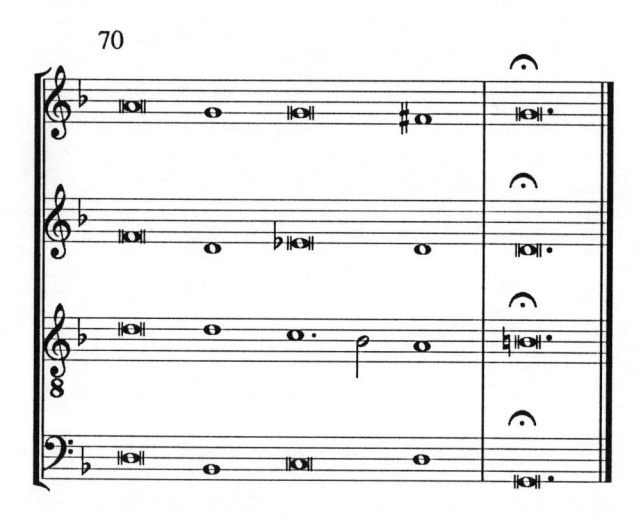

152 CANZON VIGESIMA, LA FURUGADA

21. Canzon vigesimaprima, La Pessa

154 Canzon vigesimaprima, La Pessa

CANZON VIGESIMAPRIMA, LA PESSA 155

156 CANZON VIGESIMAPRIMA, LA PESSA

CANZON VIGESIMAPRIMA, LA PESSA 157

Canzon vigesimaprima, La Pessa

CANZON VIGESIMAPRIMA, LA PESSA 159

160 CANZON VIGESIMAPRIMA, LA PESSA

CONTENTS OF THE SERIES

Volume 1
Giuliano Tiburtino, Adriano Willaert, Cipriano de Rore, Baldassare Donato, and Nadal
Fantasie, et recerchari a tre voci (Venice, 1549)

Volume 2
Adriano Willaert, Antonino Barges, Girolamo Cavazzoni, Cipriano de Rore, and anonymous
Fantasie recercari contrapunti a tre voci (Venice, 1551)

Volume 3
Jacques Buus
Il secondo libro di recercari . . . a quatro voci (Venice, 1549)

Volume 4
Annibale Padovano
Il primo libro de ricercari a quattro voci (Venice, 1556)

Volumes 5–7
Claudio Merulo
Il primo libro de ricercari da cantare, a quattro voci (Venice, 1574)
Ricercari da cantare a quattro voci . . . libro secondo (Venice, 1607)
Ricercari da cantare a quattro voci . . . libro terzo (Venice, 1608)

Volume 8
Giovanni Bassano
Fantasie a tre voci, per cantar et sonar con ogni sorte d'istrumenti (Venice, 1585)
Andrea Gabrieli
Madrigali et ricercari . . . a quattro voci (Venice, 1589)

Valerio Bona
Il secondo libro delle canzonette a tre voci con l'aggionta di dodeci tercetti a note (Venice, 1592)

Volume 9
Florentio Maschera
Libro primo de canzoni . . . a quattro voci (Brescia, 1584)

Volume 10
Canzon di diversi . . . a quatro cinque, & sei voci . . . libro primo (Venice, 1588)
Giovanni Cavaccio
Musica . . . ove si contengono due fantasie . . . canzoni alla franzese, pavana co'l saltarello, madrigali, & un proverbio . . . a quattro voci (Venice, 1597)

Volume 11
Francesco (Sponga) Usper
Ricercari et arie francesi à quattro voci (Venice, 1595)

Volume 12
Ottavio Bariolla
Capricci overo canzoni à quattro . . . libro terzo (Milan, 1594)

Volume 13
Antonio Mortaro
Primo libro de canzoni da sonare a quattro voci (Venice, 1600)

Volume 14
Floriano Canale
Canzoni da sonare a quattro, et otto voci . . . libro primo (Venice, 1600)

Volume 15
Paolo Quagliati
Recercate, et canzone . . . libro primo à quattro voci (Rome, 1601)

Volume 16
Giovanni Domenico Rognoni Taeggio
Canzoni à 4. & 8. voci . . . libro primo (Milan, 1605)

Volume 17
Antonio Troilo
Il primo libro delle canzoni . . . a quatro et cinque voci (Venice, 1606)

Volume 18
Adriano Banchieri
Fantasie overo canzoni alla francese . . . a quattro voci (Venice, 1603)
Ascanio Mayone
Primo libro di ricercari a tre voci (Naples, 1606)

Volume 19
Agostino Soderini
Canzoni à 4. & 8. voci . . . libro primo (Milan, 1608)

Volume 20
Cesario Gussago
Sonate a quattro, sei, et otti (Venice, 1608)

Volume 21 (two books)
Lodovico Viadana
Sinfonie musicali a otto voci (Venice, 1610)

Volume 22
Francesco Rovigo and Ruggier Trofeo
Canzoni da suonare à quattro, et à otto (Milan, [1613?])

Volume 23
Stefano Bernardi
Motetti in cantilena a quattro voci, con alcune canzoni (Venice, 1613)

Concerti academici con varia sorte di sinfonie . . . libro primo (Venice, 1615)

Volume 24
Giovanni Antonio Cangiasi
Scherzi forastieri per suonare a quattro voci (Milan, 1614)

Volume 25
Johann Hieronymus Kapsberger
Libro primo de balli, gagliarde, et correnti, a quattro voci (Rome, 1615)
Libro primo di sinfonie a quattro (Rome, 1615)

Volume 26
Pietro Lappi
Canzoni da suonare . . . a 4. 5. 6. 7. 8. 9. 10. 11. 12. & 13, libro primo (Venice, 1616)

Volume 27
Lorenzo Allegri
Il primo libro delle musiche (Venice, 1618)

Volume 28
Giovanni Battista Grillo
Sacri concentus ac symphoniae . . . 6. 7. 8. 12. voc. (Venice, 1618)

Volume 29
Francesco Lucino (ed.)
Seconda aggiunta alli concerti . . . di diversi eccellenti autori . . . con . . . dodeci canzoni per sonare (Milan, 1617)
Nicolò Corradini
Primo libro de canzoni francese a 4. & alcune suonate (Venice, 1624)

Volume 30
Giacomo Filippo Biumi
Canzoni alla francese à 4. & à 8. con alcune arie de correnti à 4 . . . libro primo (Milan, 1627)